Phases and Rooms

BY

REVEREND RICKY EDWARDS

FORWARD

Phases and Rooms is a book written to help leadership, Ministry of helps and the five fold ministers to complete the full redemptive plan that God has for our life. Brother Hagin used to say that "many ministers never get out of their first phase of ministry" This is a tragedy in todays day and age. It has become ever so important as that time nears Jesus's return for us to be effective and finish the race that God has prepared for us.

It's an Honor and a Privilege to be asked to write the forward for Phases and Rooms. As my spiritual father, Rev. Ricky Edwards has proven to be instrumental through his help, guidance, and insight for my development and success in my life and ministry. A few ministers had asked if Rev. Ricky was willing to do a conference on this subject and this book has been adapted from that conference which was held with key leadership at Stonepoint Community Church in Peoria, Arizona. This book will truly be a blessing to you. This book takes a biblical look at the development of the call of God upon our lives. We as ministers have much to accomplish in the ministry God has given us. Whether you are in the Ministry of helps, the five fold ministry and especially if you are just starting out; this book will bring light, illumination, and revelation to the full redemptive plan that God has for our life and ministry. Integrity and character have become punchlines and cliches in the society we live in. However, in these end times never has teaching on the subject been more needed. Effective leadership has to be developed out of the art of following.

If you have a deep hunger and are after the perfect will of God concerning your ministry then this book will prove to be an invaluable tool that beckons to be read over and over again gleaning the invaluable nuggets and revelations.

Gene Herndon
Stonepoint Community Church
Senior Pastor

TABLE OF CONTENTS

Chapter 1: Phases for the Five Fold Ministry

1 Corinthians 12:28

And God hath set some in the church, first apostles, secondarily prophets, thirdly teachers, after that miracles, then gifts of healings, helps, governments, diversities of tongues.

Many will agree that all the gifts listed in verse 28 are ministry gifts. They are not the gifts of the Spirit. The gifts of the Spirit are found in the beginning. Here we see then that a teacher is a ministry gift, as are the gifts of miracles and gifts of healings.

In 1980, in Fredrick KC Price's church, Brother Hagin (Keneth E. Hagin) taught about the 4 phases of ministry and went into special gifts. That teaching was given to him out of Hebrews 2:4, as an endowment. That teaching explains some things about what we are endeavoring to get out to the Body of Christ.

So he says, "God has set some in the church, first apostles, secondarily prophet, thirdly teachers, after that, miracles, gifts of healings." Many times people will put emphasis on the apostle, prophet, pastor, evangelists and teacher. Those five are listed in Ephesians 4. But if this is a list of ministry gifts, helps is right smack dab in the middle of it. That is why I always like to say there is no such animal as a music ministry. Under the guidelines of the ministry of helps, you will find music flowing there. But, it is not a separate ministry that will stand on its own; it is a ministry to come alongside of the other five. But if there are rooms, or phases and rooms for the other 5 ministry gifts, then there must be rooms and phases or phases and rooms in the ministry of helps. And if we need to get to all of them to finish our course, then, we hve got to figure out where we are right now, where we are supposed to be serving. Because, it is key to live long enough so we can say like the Apostle Paul, "I have kept the faith, I have kept the Word God gave me, I finished my course, I finished every phase and every room, henceforth there is laid up for me a crown of righteousness." If Pastors understand this, then ministry of helps will be helped with this.

Romans 12:1-2

1 I beseech you therefore, brethren, by the mercies of God, that ye present your bodies a living sacrifice, holy, acceptable unto God, which is your reasonable service.

2 And be not conformed to this world: but be ye transformed by the renewing of your mind, that ye may prove what is that good, and acceptable, and perfect, will of God.

So in Romans 12:1-2, Paul writes here to the Church of Rome but also to the church wherever you are from. He says, "I beseech you therefore Brethren by the mercies of God, that you present your bodies, a living sacrifice, holy, acceptable unto God, which is your reasonable service. And, be not conformed to this world, but be transformed by the renewing of your mind, so that you may prove what is that Good, acceptable, and perfect will of God." Now we know that it is also recorded... it is talked about... the good, and where it says "acceptable" some translations will say "permissible" and then others will say, "perfect." King James says, "perfect will of God." So, the good, acceptable, and perfect will of God.

When Brother Hagin was ministering, he pastored for 12 straight years then travelled for 3. Then Jesus appeared to him, and said at that time, "You are just now entering into the first phase of your ministry." And he said, "Lord, I know I did not hear your right." This account is mentioned in both books: *I Believe in Visions* and *Understanding the Anointing*. He said, "Lord I know I did not hear you right. I have been pastoring 12 years and I have travelled and ministered for three. What do you mean I just now am getting into the first phase of my ministry?" Now in the book *Understanding the Anointing* this is what Jesus said to him, "Many of my ministers live and die, and never get into the first phase of their ministry. Many never live out half of what they were called out to live, and the reason is, they never get into where I called them." So He told him, He said, "You have only been in my permissive will," but he said, "I desire for you now to find where I called you to, to get into my perfect will."

1 Peter 5:10

But the God of all grace, who hath called us unto his eternal glory by Christ Jesus, after that ye have suffered a while, make you perfect, stablish, strengthen, settle you.

In another one of Brother Hagin's books, *Must Christians Suffer?* he states that we aught to never suffer with things that Jesus bore for us as our savior, as our substitute. Jesus took sin, sickness and disease, poverty and lack. I sure am glad we do not have to suffer with that. Where he was our example, we are supposed to walk like him.

3

However, the permissive will of God is never wasted time. 1 Peter 5:10 tells us, "After you have suffered awhile, that you may be established." The Lord Jesus told bother Hagin, "The years that you pastored and endured, out of that, if you had not been able to go through the smaller things back then, you would have never been able to really go through what I have actually called you to go into." Brother Hagin believed he was so established and that the storms of life did not bother him, all because of all the things he had suffered. It was not what Jesus bore for him, but the things he suffered in the early days learning the Ministry.

In another illustration, a woman received a vision from God about going to China. He showed her, as she went to china, that she would have a ministry. He showed her a vision that she would have 1,000 children. She was there for 10 years and only had 100 kids. Finally she said, "Lord, I missed you, or I am not doing something right, I need to know how come I do not have the thousand children." He said, "The reason you only have 100 children is because I had to make sure you would stay through the hard times. If, the first year you got here, I had given you 1,000 and it was too hard and you would have left," he said, "I would have had a thousand children that would have thought I was a God who would not take care of them. The hundred are precious to me but I can deal with 100 easier than I can with a thousand. But you have been found faithful; I know you are not going to run." This is what he also said, "You are made of the right stuff." So he said, "Now you get your thousand."

It is like when we would go to bible school and Brother Hagin would tell us, or different ministers would tell us, "It will take 2 years before I will license, or ordain you." "Because, (he would say), the book says, (in the book of Timothy Paul writes), 'let a minister prove himself'." That means we need time to get to certain places. These are all illustrations and samples of progression.

I remember when we were all in bible school; there were some young men, who use to tell everyone they were prophets. They were also in their mid 20s and 30s, not nearly old enough yet. Just because you can sense the call, does it qualify you? You are only called, but you are not ready. Some of us that are getting a little older now, are finally getting to an age where God can begin to use us some; not that he has not used us in the past. We learn and grow as we go through some things.

We are certainly glad for the good and acceptable will of God, but we are after the perfect will of God. Sure now, when we are first starting out, or as we are growing, we aught not feel bad if we are not where we know we are going to end up, but rejoice. Here is the key; we have got to live long enough to finish. We have got to live long enough to finish this thing,

1949 was the year Brother Hagin entered into the first phase of his ministry, and he had been preaching for 15 years. He went through that phase in 12 months. The second phase took him 8 months. The third phase, he stayed in it until June of 1979, over 25 years. Now this detail is important, because the last time when Jesus appeared to him, He told him this; He said, "If you will be faithful, I will appear to you one more time, and at that time, you will enter into your fourth and final phase." That ought to give us a heads up; this thing is conditional, and

I have got to live long enough to get there. That is just not for preachers. If the ministry of helps is in the list with the preachers, then we need to be teaching the ministry of helps. There ought to be a progression, there ought to be some growth. God is not looking for stars; he is looking for people from whom to make super-stars. And, if you are ever caught and found faithful, God wants to promote you. Try pushing your way to the top. It will be a struggle, but you just stay faithful to what God has called you to be. God will make sure that you get promoted.

In June of 1979, Jesus had told him, "If you are faithful, I will appear to you one more time. At that time, you will enter into your fourth, and final phase of ministry." It is important to mention that twice before that time, Brother Hagin almost died. He kept getting away from the thing God had called him to do. It is good to mention here that this is why this book is geared towards ministry leaders; we do not have to explain to people, "You mean God was going to kill him?" No, God is not hurting anyone, but if you get away from what God has called you to do, you get out of the perfect plan and you get over into the permissive. There the devil will smack you! He will hit you hard and sometimes it hurts!

Hebrews 6:2-3

2 Of the doctrine of baptisms, and of laying on of hands, and of resurrection of the dead, and of eternal judgment.

3 And this will we do, if God permit.

In 1988 my wife, Sally, and I left Rhema. We went, and we ended up in Silsbee Texas with a bible study. And then in 1992, the Lord began to deal with me about going out once a month, or once every 2 or 3 months, and he said, "I will give you a specific message according to Hebrews Chapter 6, verses 2 and 3," and He said, "Anything that has begun to wane, I will revive." A revival is something that has had a "vive" at one time, but needs to be "re-vived." And He said, "I will give you a message, and I will send you to different places." And he said, "Do not make a lot of push to call people." And not at that time, but he said, "I will send you."

So we started. Then in 1994, 1995 a few of the ministers where I had preached over the process of the previous three or four years told me, "If you will calm down, we will have you back." And so, I just said, "Well Lord, I will tell you what," because it hurt my feelings. So I sulked for a while, and I pouted. All of a sudden, I started getting symptoms in my body, and I ended up bed ridden. This was 1996; and I became bedridden and I could not get out of the bed to get to the bathroom. I could not walk; I had to have help, different things. And in this process of time, I said, "Lord, I need help here!" So some of the deacons, or elders came by, and they said, "We have come to pray with you." I said, "I do not want you to pray with me; I am too sick to pray; pray for me." Well they all prayed and mustered up all the faith they could, and of course we did not get any better than nowhere. We were still passing blood, different things, and so finally my wife and I got together and we said, "Lord, we have got to know something, what is up? What is going on?" And, He said, "What are you going to do about travelling?" Now I said, "Lord I really was not planning on doing much about it. But if I am not going to get out of this bed, I will go." The reason we are directing this teaching towards leaders is because people will twist stuff like this. Leaders will not because you understand what is going on. God does not hurt people, but if we get off of God's perfect will, we will get off into the enemy's territory. So my wife and I made the adjustments, and we got things squared away, and we took off and went after it again.

In the process of time, here is something that began to transpire and something that began to manifest. I began to get glimpses of the future. I began to see really what God was calling me into. We had been preaching since 1987. Here we were up into 1996; we had left Silsbee and had gone back to Oklahoma; we had booked up and started travelling full time. Then we began to get glimpses of some things ahead of our future. You get glimpses; God will let you taste and see things that are out ahead of you. David wrote and said, "Oh taste and see that the Lord is good." I do not know if you have ever experienced this or not, but there will be times in the earlier days, when you will have a service and it will be like a blowout; I mean the power of God, the Glory Cloud, people will be piled up like cordwood everywhere, and you will have services like that, and you are like, "DEAR GOD HOW CAN I GET THEM BACK?" He has let you taste of what is ahead of you to keep you hungry. But we are not ready to flow in all of that at that time. But he will let you taste of it.

Romans 12:3

For I say, through the grace given unto me, to every man that is among you, not to think of himself more highly than he ought to think; but to think soberly, according as God hath dealt to every man the measure of faith.

So, we began to get glimpses of the future. We began to be able to taste of some things. In Romans 12:3, Paul writes and says, "For I say through the grace, given unto me, to every man that is among you, not

8

think of himself more highly than he ought to think, but to think soberly according as God hath dealt to every man the measure of faith." Has God given every man the ability for a measure of faith? There are two things here. Now notice it says, "For I say through the grace given unto me."

Ephesians 3:7

Whereof I was made a minister, according to the gift of the grace of God given unto me by the effectual working of his power.

Let us recall that in Ephesians 3:7, Paul says this, "Wherefore I was made a minister according to the gift of the grace of God given unto me by the effectual working of his power." If that is true, how did this gift come, or through what? It came through grace.

Ephesians 4:7

But unto every one of us is given grace according to the measure of the gift of Christ.

Ephesians 4:7 says, "But unto every one of us is given grace according to your supply." Your supply to the body will always flow through your measure. So, at this point we can agree that we are what we are by the grace of God. In 1 Corinthians 15, Paul did not say that, by meaning this, that God was going to put him in a Half-Nelson and make him be an apostle to the gentiles whether he wanted to be or not. No, he did not say that. He yielded to the grace of God; and by yielding to the grace of God he became what God called him to be.

Romans 12:3

For I say, through the grace given unto me, to every man that is among you, not to think of himself more highly than he ought to think; but to

think soberly, according as God hath dealt to every man the measure of faith.

Romans 12:3 says, "For I say through the grace given."

John 1:17

For the law was given by Moses, but grace and truth came by Jesus Christ.

And if we recall the law came by Moses; grace and truth came through, or by Jesus Christ. So all of a sudden then, this grace is only available in the church age because it came by Jesus. Paul said he was a minister by the grace and he said, "According to the grace given, and the measure." Look at Romans 12:3 again. "For I say through the grace given unto me."

Ephesians 2:8

For by grace are ye saved through faith; and that not of yourselves: it is the gift of God:

We know this; Ephesians 2:8 says, "For by grace are you saved through faith." So we get into what grace has provided through faith.

Romans 5:2

By whom also we have access by faith into this grace wherein we stand, and rejoice in hope of the glory of God.

"Wherefore, we have access by faith into this grace." Is that right? We access our church, hospital, school or whatever buildings by the door, correct? Similarly, whatever the grace of God has on your life to do, you are still going to have to access it by the faith of God. So, if God will give you a glimpse of what is ahead of you in your future, just because the grace of God is on you, does not mean you will get there.

You are still going to have to go after it by faith. If people said, "I do not know if I can do that." You do not do it in an area where heathens are concerned. When you have sickness in your body, you will stand up and say, "By the stripes of Jesus I am healed!" You will say things that are according to the word of God, even though it is not that way in your life naturally because you do not want what you have. You do not say what you have, you say what the word of God says you can have, and that is what you are going after. God will give you glimpses of your future concerning the grace that is upon your life, but it takes faith to reach out and grab it!

Hebrews 12, there are some truths here in these phrases. What I want you to understand is that when it is all tied in together, it will make more sense about the grace of God on your life and what God has called you to do.

Hebrews 12:15

Looking diligently lest any man fail of the grace of God; lest any root of bitterness springing up trouble you, and thereby many be defiled;

Going to Hebrews 12:15 we read: "Looking diligently, lest any man fail," I will say, 'fall from', "fall from the grace of God, lest any root of bitterness springing up trouble, you and thereby many be defiled." Can we fall from grace? To fall from grace does not mean one falls and loses his salvation. Paul said he was made a minister by the grace. The law came through Moses, grace and truth by Jesus Christ.

Ephesians 4:8

Wherefore he saith, When he ascended up on high, he led captivity captive, and gave gifts unto men.

Ephesians 4:8 says that Jesus lead captivity captive, and gave gifts unto men, and therefore there is a measure given to every man by the head of the church."

How would one fall from grace? How does one get into grace? One gets into grace by faith. So, the only way to fall from grace is to no longer access it by faith because the only way to get into grace is... through faith.

Mark 11:20-22

20And in the morning, as they passed by, they saw the fig tree dried up from the roots.

21And Peter calling to remembrance saith unto him, Master, behold, the fig tree which thou cursedst is withered away.

22And Jesus answering saith unto them, Have faith in God.

Mark 11:20. You know that we need to know how to answer stuff when it talks to you negatively concerning what God has told you to do. Verse 20, "And in the morning as they passed by, they saw the fig tree dried up from the roots, and Peter calling into remembrance, saith unto him, 'Master, behold the fig tree which thou cursed is withered away' and Jesus answering saith unto them, "have faith in God." In my bible I got a little note that says, "Have the faith of God." So have the faith of God, or have faith where in God. How can one have the faith of God? His word! So the only way to have the God kind of faith is to have the God kind of Word.

Romans 10:17

So then faith cometh by hearing, and hearing by the word of God.

Romans 10:17 says, "So then faith cometh by…hearing, and …hearing by the … word of God." So whatever part of the word I heard that I will believe. Hearing is in there twice, so the Lord asked me, "How come that is in there twice?" I said, "I do not know" and he said, "Whatever part of the word that you have heard that you will believe will always qualify as faith."

It is not that people, when Jesus preached, did not hear what he said; they just did not believe what he said. So he said, "He that hath ears to hear, let him hear." So whatever part of the message you preach, that people in your congregation will actually believe, will always qualify as faith. Sometime people think just hearing the word is faith. No, that is not what it says. So then, you take this all of a sudden right here, the only way to have the God kind of faith, or have faith in God, is to have a God kind of word.

Romans 12:3

For I say, through the grace given unto me, to every man that is among you, not to think of himself more highly than he ought to think; but to think soberly, according as God hath dealt to every man the measure of faith.

You can have faith in other things. In Romans 12: 3 He says, "But to think soberly according as God has dealt to every man the measure of faith." So we have to ask if there is the ability for every man to have the measure of a God kind of faith.

2 Thessalonians 3:2

And that we may be delivered from unreasonable and wicked men: for all men have not faith.

But 2 Thessalonians 3:2 says, "So that we might be delivered from unreasonable and wicked men for all men have not faith." Yet, Romans 12:3 says that God has given to every man a measure of faith. However, 2 Thessalonians says that, "all men have not faith." So, the only way to have the God kind of faith is to have a God kind of word. David wrote and said, "Some trust in chariots, and others have put their faith in," faith in the economy or whatever else. But, the only way to have the God kind of faith is to have the God kind of word. Because faith cometh by hearing and whatever part of God's word I heard, that what I believe will always qualify as the God kind of faith. I can have faith in other things, but the only way to have a God kind of faith is to have the God kind of word.

Romans 14:23

And he that doubteth is damned if he eat, because he eateth not of faith: for whatsoever is not of faith is sin.

So, in Romans 14:23, it talks about the beginning, "whosoever eateth, eateth not" and all that. But, then he says at the end of verse 23, "but whatsoever is not of faith is sin," the God kind, the God kind of faith. So whatsoever is not of faith, is sin.

When Paul said, "I have kept the, faith," paraphrasing he he was saying "I kept the word God gave me when he called me, and I never let trouble cause me to back out of faith, so there I was able to finish my course."

Hebrews 12:15

Looking diligently lest any man fail of the grace of God; lest any root of bitterness springing up trouble you, and thereby many be defiled;

14

So he says in Hebrews 12:15, "Looking diligently, lest any man does fail of the grace." My bible in the margins says, "fall from." Other translations have, "come short of." There are several different ones, "come short of, fall from, fall short of the Grace of God." You and I only get into the grace of God by faith. To fall from grace I would have to back out of whatever word I really believed was God. So, ministers many times will say, "I am just burnt out, I do not know, I am going to quit!" It is not that they fall from grace; they quit having faith in the word that got them there.

A quick example: My wife and I were raised in a denomination. Mom and Dad loved God. They were good parents. When Mom died, I remember that I would not trust God in the area of healing because I thought God could have healed, but would not do it. We were told that if Mom got healed then we needed her more than God, but if she did not get healed, then God needed her more than us, kids. Nobody was trying to hurt us. That is just how they rationalized it. They were not trying to hurt or destroy, but I took it in the wrong way. So in the area of healing, I would never access what the grace of God provided, because I did not trust God or have any faith there; however, everything of life is provided by the grace of God, and it takes faith to enter every area that grace has provided. So I fell from grace in the area of healing because I would not trust God.

Romans 12:3

For I say, through the grace given unto me, to every man that is among you, not to think of himself more highly than he ought to think; but to think soberly, according as God hath dealt to every man the measure of faith.

But then, in Romans 12:3 Paul says that he was given a measure of grace and called to preach, and you have got to have faith in the word God gave you, because that is all that will be steady when all hell is breaking loose! That is what causes some to question their call, or to leave their call because they leave the word; God does not leave!

Hebrews 12:15

Looking diligently lest any man fail of the grace of God; lest any root of bitterness springing up trouble you, and thereby many be defiled;

Going back to Hebrews 12:15, he says, "Looking diligently, lest any man fail of the grace of God." When a worker comes up and says, "Pastor, I am telling you what. I just feel like the grace has lifted off of me to work with the kids." If the word of God has not changed, then we are going to have to move back over into faith about that word because we access what grace has provided through faith.

Romans 12:2-3

2 And be not conformed to this world: but be ye transformed by the renewing of your mind, that ye may prove what is that good, and acceptable, and perfect, will of God.

3 For I say, through the grace given unto me, to every man that is among you, not to think of himself more highly than he ought to think; but to think soberly, according as God hath dealt to every man the measure of faith.

Romans 12:2 says, "be not conformed to this world, be ye transformed by the renewing of your mind that you may prove what is the good, acceptable and perfect will of God. For I say, through the grace given unto me to every man that is among you, not to think of himself more highly than he ought." But if God called you to be a Pastor and somebody asks, "What do you do?" If you answer, "I am a Pastor," are you thinking more highly of yourself than you ought to? If somebody says, "Well, how are you in your standing with God?" and you stand up and say, "I am the righteousness of God in Christ Jesus!" Are you thinking more highly of yourself than you ought to? Whatever the grace of God is on you for, you are not exalting yourself, you are not.

There are some pastors with whom I am close who will want to help; they will want to open doors; they will want to carry my stuff; All of that is good. In reality, we are all just equal together as far as being human beings. I do understand the honoring of the office, though; I understand that. However, usually you do not have to tell everybody, "Quit thinking so highly of yourself!" Usually you have to be pumping everybody up in the body of Christ to even get them to know who they are in Christ. But I am talking to key people; I am talking to leadership. You ought to know who you are in Christ, and you do know!

So he said, "not to think more highly of himself." If you are called to preach and somebody asks you, you tell them, "I am a minister of the gospel, glory to God!" Some ask me, "Well what are you called to?" I say, "I am not completely sure yet, because I am still growing. Right now, I just travel." I mean seriously; I am only in my early 50s! I am still a young feller!

Romans 12:6

Having then gifts differing according to the grace that is given to us, whether prophecy, let us prophesy according to the proportion of faith;

Going back to verse 3: "For I say to the grace given unto me, to every man that is among you, not to think of himself more highly that he ought, but, to think soberly, according as God has dealt to every man the measure of faith." Now verse 6, "Having then gifts differing according to the proportion of faith." So the grace qualifies the gift. Grace came into the family of God through Jesus Christ. The Law came through Moses.

"Having then gifts differing according to the grace that is given unto us." When somebody like me. I pastored with my wife from 1988 to 2008. I started travelling full time in 2008. I pastured with her all those years and still do when I am home, but I am not the Pastor anymore. The grace did not lift, but the word of God changed. So therefore if the word of God is changing, there is a different grace. I hope that makes sense. And what happens many times, in times of transition, people get frustrated because they are not "this" anymore, and they are not "that" yet. And they get frustrated because you are, if I can say it this way, "in limbo."

So when you are in the ministry of helps, and you have been faithful, and you have been, let us say ushering, and you just worked diligently, you helped established ushers, and I mean you have been faithful, faithful, faithful, and God talks to the Pastor and says, "Alright I want you to promote them, I want them now to do this." Then he comes to you and he says, "The Lord told me you are not ushering anymore, now you are this." The highest office in the local church is the office of a shepherd. Let me repeat that; the highest office in the local church is the office of a shepherd. It is not a guest speaker, it is, the office of a shepherd. And, every guest speaker that comes in should always be submitted to the highest office in that body, and that is the office of the shepherd. That is the highest office there. So, the Pastor says, "I believe this, this, this, this." It is not that you fail from grace, but he heard from heaven, he will minister or talk to you about it. He is giving you time to check with your heart; trust your leadership in this way as we trust God.

It is that the word has changed; it is not that you fail from grace; there is now a different grace. Sometimes, between the transitional period, people get frustrated because they are familiar, because they have flowed in a certain area and they are familiar with that. So every time God asks them to move out it is new water and they are like, "Oh God I do not know, I do not know that office." So we will jump back to where we are familiar. But, take the time to study some things.

1 Corinthians 16:9

For a great door and effectual is opened unto me, and there are many adversaries.

In 1 Corinthians 16:9 it says, "There is a door that is effectual," and it has great benefits, so when you get ready to step through it, know this, every time you go through an open door, there are many adversaries at the door to keep you from going through it and keep you from staying in it!

Romans 12:6-8

6 Having then gifts differing according to the grace that is given to us, whether prophecy, let us prophesy according to the proportion of faith;

7 Or ministry, let us wait on our ministering: or he that teacheth, on teaching;

8 Or he that exhorteth, on exhortation: he that giveth, let him do it with simplicity; he that ruleth, with diligence; he that sheweth mercy, with cheerfulness.

So verse 6 says, "Having then gifts differing according to the grace that is given to us for the prophecy that is prophesy according to a proportion of faith. Ministry… let us wait on our ministry, or he that teacheth, on teaching, exhorteth, on exhortation." This is grace on people. The only way to get into what grace has provided is through faith, by faith.

The gifts according to grace that is given 2 us:

1) prophecy - according 2 our proporation (measure?) of faith

2) ministry - wait on our ministering

3) teaching

4) exhortation

5) gives - do it w/ simplicity

6) rules - w/ diligence

7) shows mercy - w/ cheerfulness

Chapter 2: The Anointing Upon

We know from studying the scripture and listening to people that have helped teach us, by the spirit, that in the old covenant, the anointing was on three groups of people. The anointing was upon the prophet, priest and king. And whoever else God would choose. Would you agree that the anointing was only *upon* in the old covenant? In the new covenant we understand that the anointing can be within, and then after the anointing comes within, then the anointing also will come upon. In Kenneth E. Hagin's book, *Understand the Anointing*, on page 139, Brother Hagin says this, "Every born-again spirit-filled believer has a measure of the spirit, and anointing within according to 1 John 2:27. But this personal anointing that is within will never be increased." There is nothing in the scripture that indicates you can have a double portion of your personal anointing or the anointing within. Yet, Elisha, when he had helped served Elijah, and Elijah prepared to go, did ask for a double portion. So the anointing upon can increase. Which is only for service.

John 4:7-10

7There cometh a woman of Samaria to draw water: Jesus saith unto her, Give me to drink.

21

8(For his disciples were gone away unto the city to buy meat.)

9Then saith the woman of Samaria unto him, How is it that thou, being a Jew, askest drink of me, which am a woman of Samaria? for the Jews have no dealings with the Samaritans.

10Jesus answered and said unto her, If thou knewest the gift of God, and who it is that saith to thee, Give me to drink; thou wouldest have asked of him, and he would have given thee living water.

John chapter 4, verse 7 says, "There cometh the woman of Samaria to draw water, and Jesus saith unto her, "give me to drink." Verse 8, "For his disciples were gone away unto the city to buy meat. Then saith the woman of Samaria unto him, 'How is it that thou being a Jew, ask a drink of me, which am a woman of Samaria, for the Jews have no dealings with the Samaritans.' Jesus answered and said unto her, 'If thou knewest the gift of God and who it is that saith to thee 'give me to drink' thou wouldst have asked of him and he would have given thee living water."

John 4:11-15

11The woman saith unto him, Sir, thou hast nothing to draw with, and the well is deep: from whence then hast thou that living water?

12Art thou greater than our father Jacob, which gave us the well, and drank thereof himself, and his children, and his cattle?

13Jesus answered and said unto her, Whosoever drinketh of this water shall thirst again:

14But whosoever drinketh of the water that I shall give him shall never thirst; but the water that I shall give him shall be in him a well of water springing up into everlasting life.

15The woman saith unto him, Sir, give me this water, that I thirst not, neither come hither to draw.

Then, "The woman saith unto him, 'Sir, thou has nothing to draw with, the well is deep, from whence then hath thou that living water?" Or, where are you going to get it from? You do not have anything to draw with. Then He says, "Art thou greater than our father Jacob which gave us the well and drank thereof himself, and his children, his cattle? Jesus answered and said unto her, 'Whosoever drinketh of this water," and I am pretty sure Jesus must have pointed at the well. And if he did point at the well, he said, "whosoever drinketh of this water shall thirst again." Verse 14 says, "But whosoever drinketh of the water that I shall give him shall never thirst; but the water that I shall give him shall be in him a well of water springing up into everlasting life." If Jesus pointed at the well, and said that whoever drinks from that hole in the ground, right there, that well, they are going to thirst again.

We all drank water yesterday or this morning from a bottle or fountain or something. We drank some natural water then and we are going to drink some more water today? Jesus said that whoever drinks of the natural water will thirst again. But he also said, "If you knew who I was and the gift I am offering, you would have asked of me and I would have given unto you living water." He said, "that will turn into a well of living water springing up into everlasting life. So the well on the inside of every born-again believer is only for you and I to drink from. The well on the inside, and if I can say it this way, the anointing on the inside, the well on the inside, is only for me to drink from.

John 14:26

23

But the Comforter, which is the Holy Ghost, whom the Father will send in my name, he shall teach you all things, and bring all things to your remembrance, whatsoever I have said unto you.

In John chapter 14, verse 26, it says, "but the comfort to which is the Holy Ghost, whom the father will send in my name," in my authority, Jesus said, "he shall teach you all things, bring all things to remembrance whatsoever I have said unto you." The amplified will bring out several other names for the word comforter: paraclete. Notice some of the things; the Holy Ghost is on the inside; he is a teacher; he is a guide.

1 John 2:27

But the anointing which ye have received of him abideth in you, and ye need not that any man teach you: but as the same anointing teacheth you of all things, and is truth, and is no lie, and even as it hath taught you, ye shall abide in him.

In 1 John 2:37 we have, "But the anointing, which you have received of Him, abideth in you, and you need not that any man teach you: but as a same anointing teacheth you of all things; and is truth, is no lie, even as it taught you, you shall abide within." And, is there anointing upon? The well on the inside of you and I is only for you and I to drink from. The anointing within is designed to do several things. It is to teach us; it is to train us; it is to help develop character in us.

The reason I am going this way is for the reason I am about to share. I was in the cab of my pickup one night at about 1:00 a.m. and the presence of God filled up the cab of my truck; he talked to me about developing character, and he talked to me about a greater degree of an anointing upon, but he said, "You have got to understand some things about measures, phases and rooms. What the anointing within is designed to do is to develop character; it is to train you, and it is to develop you." Because to whom much is given, much is required. So if you are looking for a greater degree of an anointing upon, the anointing within is to help keep you there so when you do get a greater degree upon, you can live healthy, prosperous, and it will not hurt you; it will be a blessing to you. So the anointing within is to teach, to train, to develop character.

John 7:37-39

37In the last day, that great day of the feast, Jesus stood and cried, saying, If any man thirst, let him come unto me, and drink.

38He that believeth on me, as the scripture hath said, out of his belly shall flow rivers of living water.

39(But this spake he of the Spirit, which they that believe on him should receive: for the Holy Ghost was not yet given; because that Jesus was not yet glorified.)

In John chapter 7 verse 37 it says, "In the last day, that great day of the feast," what did Jesus say? "If any man thirst, let him come to me, and drink." That is the well. Verse 38 says, "He that believeth on me as the scripture has said out of his belly, shall flow rivers of living water. But this spake He of the spirit which they that believed on Him should receive, for the Holy Ghost was not yet given because Jesus was not yet glorified." The well, or the anointing within, is for you and I to drink from. The river is a flow that is for service.

When Sally and I were in South East Texas, we became acquainted with an older minister; he was in the Assemblies of God, and was, I believe, a true apostle of his calling. Jesus had appeared to him, I believe several times over the course of some years. I still remember when he told me that Jesus appeared to him, we talked for over 45 minutes. This man had had angels appeared to him; he had established 7 Assembly of God Churches that are all still going to this day. He was also the one that had Brother Hagin come to minister for when Brother Hagin left his last church and went out on the field ministry. He was one of the very first to have him come and do a meeting for him. He had also had some people from the dead raised up, blind healed, deaf healed, crippled walk and different things. So, this is what he had said to me one day, "Everything you can find in scripture," he said, "I have seen happen under my ministry." But, he had begun to develop congestive heart failure. And so, he or his wife, a lot of times, would call us because he began to struggle for breath. So we would go and we would pray for him. So one of the nights that we were there, he said, "Brother Ricky," he said, "I want to ask you a question." He went on, "I have seen the dead raised; I have seen the blind eyes open; I have seen the deaf hear; I have seen all of these things, but," he said, "what I cannot figure out is how come God will not heal me of congestive heart failure?" Well, I knew when he said that, not because I am so smart, but because I paid attention to Brother Hagin under the anointing; I knew that what had happened was that he had learned to cooperate with the river, which is only for service. He thought he could drink from the river. You as a minister, you cannot drink from whatever degree of an anointing God has put on you for service; you must learn to drink from the well God has put in you. We all have to drink from the well, but I cannot drink from the river that is on my life for Ministry. The river is for service for the body. So he had learned to flow with the river and minister healing and all these things to the body, but he also wanted to be healed by the river. But he needed to get

26

healed by faith in the word of God, or else have some other minister pray for him.

Sometimes ministers think, "well you know, I am a Pastor," and every time we sit down to read to study, we are looking for something for the body of Christ. That will cause you to get weary because you are looking for something that will flow through the river. However, you have got to learn to drink from the well! That will keep you strong, that will keep you fresh. Do not always look for a message; out of your fellowship with God, out of your time drinking, allow the river to flow out of that.

Isaiah 10:27

And it shall come to pass in that day, that his burden shall be taken away from off thy shoulder, and his yoke from off thy neck, and the yoke shall be destroyed because of the anointing.

So this brother had begun to talk to us; he had said, "I do not understand how come God will not heal me." Remember: the river is for service that will flow through you. In Isaiah 10:27, the anointing will do two things, and I am not saying these are the only two things it will do, but Isaiah 10:27 says, the anointing will remove burdens and destroy yokes. That does not just say the anointing upon or the river.

1 John 2:27

But the anointing which ye have received of him abideth in you, and ye need not that any man teach you: but as the same anointing teacheth you of all things, and is truth, and is no lie, and even as it hath taught you, ye shall abide in him.

So If you have got an anointing within according to 1 John 2:27, as you study the word, as you look at the word, the anointing within you itself will be a teacher, a leader, a guide. That same anointing within you, as you study, as you prepare, and drink from that well, that anointing has the ability to remove burdens and destroy yokes. Amen! It is the same anointing that can come by the laying on of hands. Brother Hagin would teach us, "I got healed on my own faith, I learned to listen, to the voice of the Holy Ghost on the inside of me that would take me to the word of God!" And he endeavored to get people to rise up and be healed, from drinking from the well, but everybody is not going to be healed from the well! So we learned the anointing will do it both ways. The anointing within will heal you too. But the anointing upon, through somebody else, through a river, will heal you. The anointing within will remove burdens, but the anointing upon, through a river will also remove burdens.

So the individual drinks from the well, which is to teach, train and develop character. The river upon is for service to the people or to the body of Christ. We are not to drink from the river; the river is for service. We are to drink from the well. We have got to learn to drink from the well in greater measures.

Romans 11:29

For the gifts and calling of God are without repentance.

Every office that God calls will have to have equipment to qualify that office. When I was in the cab of the pickup, and it was 1:00 a.m. on i-40 headed west and the presence of God filled up the cab of that truck, this is what the Lord said to me, "You have been bugging me." God talks to me the way I talk, so I can understand. He said, "You have been bugging me about an increase of power." And he said, "What you have to understand," and this is what he asked me, and I

28

was glad I knew the answer, He said, "What does Romans 11:29 say?" I said, "Well, Romans 11:29 says, 'For the gifts and callings of God, are without repentance.'" Irrevocable, cannot be changed, nor taken back. He said, "You are bothering me, bugging me, about an increase of power concerning this measure where you are going into."

Before I go on, and to further illustrate, I want to share something briefly. This happened about two years ago when we were in Lockhart, Texas. The word of the Lord came and we were teaching about the 10 lepers, and how 9 of them were content to go through life with still body parts missing, but then one of them came back and was made whole. That meant everything he had lost grew back. And so, we were teaching that and the word of the Lord came and said, "There is somebody here that needs a creative miracle. Something replaced that is gone." So a lady got up and came forward, and everybody knew her and testified it was the truth; she did not have a little finger. Well, we grabbed hold of her hand and prayed, and it grew out to the first joint. Everybody was so excited and jumping and all that. I was not very impressed; I did not act disappointed or anything. I shouted with them and all, but as soon as I got away from everybody I said, "Lord I want to know something; how come I could not get the whole finger?" He said, "You are only operating at about 28%."

This takes me to the time when Brother Hagin was up in Buffalo, New York. He said that at that time, he and Sister Oretha were the only two in the ministry; he did not have anyone to help even with the book table. He had carried in the last box of books feeling like he was going to faint because he was so sick. He would tell how he had positioned himself where if he did fall he would fall over the bed. And he did fall; when he fell, Sister Oretha came running over and said, "Honey,

29

Honey, are you alright?" To that he had responded, "I am sick." And it upset her, because she said in twenty something years she had not heard him say he was sick. And so, he did get sick and the Lord dealt with him. The Lord let him know the only way he was going to get healed. The Lord told him, "Close out this meeting, go back to Tulsa, have a weeklong meeting, teach on a certain subject, and," these things happened to him but they also happened for us to glean from, he said, "the anointing you have experienced 4 times over the past 10 years," the anointing he had tasted, not been walking in, "the anointing you have tasted, or have experienced 4 times in the last 10 years will come upon you to abide." We have got increase!

So I said, "Okay, Lord." He said, "You got 28%." That is what I had been talking to the Lord about for a couple years. I said, "Lord, I need to know about some of these things?" He said, "You have been bothering me about power." And he began to talk to me, "Did you not understand that the anointing within will help develop character?" He said, "Let us say people bring in a small child and his body is completely twisted, and they bring him in, and the power of God miraculously raises that baby up and that baby runs out." He said, "Parents will throw money at you. People will want you to come. People will treat you differently than they treat you now." And he said, "You have got to grow and develop to a place where money and glory will not move you." He said, "You are going to have to stay as humble as you are right now." Remember He talked to Saul and said, "When thou was little in thine own sight"? Brother Hagin, he said, "Always, always receive correction; never receive praise!" People want to get that backwards. When they bring correction, you stick your lip out.

You want them to say, "Boy, you did a real good job." Reject praise; always be willing, open, to receive correction.

1 Corinthians 13:11

When I was a child, I spake as a child, I understood as a child, I thought as a child: but when I became a man, I put away childish things.

So the Lord said to me, "Do you not understand about character and development?" Remember, we are all at different places growing spiritually? Take 16, 17 or 18 year olds, they do not act like us that are fifty. Paul wrote in 1 Corinthians; "When I was a child, I thought like a child," I interpret everything from where I am. I acted like a child; I thought like a child; I perceived things like a child. Now that I have matured, I am still the same person, but now my interpretation is different.

Romans 11:29

For the gifts and calling of God are without repentance.

Remember, Romans 11:29 says that the gifts and callings of God are without repentance, irrevocable, cannot be taken back. The Lord said to me that night, "Do you understand that once the power increases, I can never take that back. And regardless of poor character, or if the way people start treating you moves you, I still cannot take that power back," because it is irrevocable. If popularity, fame, glory, has the ability to move us, or a lot of money comes and you change, that power still cannot be taken back. Like I mentioned previously, we are thankful people want to carry our things, open doors, that is them acknowledging the office, but not worshipping the man. I am grateful for honor, but I am still, Ricky from Pawnee, Oklahoma. Sometimes this stuff moves us. This is what God was talking to me in the cab of the truck that night, and I am sharing more than I have ever said before.

He said, "Did you notice Jack Cole or William Branham? I put my power on them. They were in a place where they were flowing really well. They had a ministry so excelled that they would take a cancer and rip it off of people's face, and brand new skin would come. Or they would line up a whole row of deaf people and they would slap them or, snap their fingers and every one of them would be instantly healed." He said, "Did you notice that their character got off. I talked to one of my servants and said, 'Go and tell him to judge himself in these areas: his love walk toward his fellow ministers and money.'" The power was on them. You have got to see that if your character gets off a little bit, the power no longer is a blessing to you. It will start working against you, because you are bringing harm to the body of Christ! Your character has to come up with the same degree of anointing upon! God said, "Do not be so anxious to have all of this on you." He continued, "You better be glad I am giving you time to grow up and develop, and come up here, because when you get there, I want you to live long enough to effectively help the body of Christ!" That is why some will rise quickly and then just be gone.

I responded, "Okay, I understand." So he said, "28%". Well I am up a little bit more since then, but I sure am not where I need to be. We need to give the anointing within time to help us. I am just glad that I have grown. I remember when I started preaching, people in the crowd would be mean-mugging me, or be mad, staring at me. And every time I would say something, they would have these expressions. Well, back then I would have been apt to respond with, "You want

32

some???" Maybe you can identify, but that was then. We are growing past that. We are not fighting anybody.

Remember when the prophet Elisha walked by a man and woman's home every day, and being that she was a smart woman, the woman watched him. She was not sucked in quickly. She watched him, perceived him and then after a period of time went to her husband and said, "Honey, I feel like we should do this, what do you think?" He said, "Sure, go ahead." So they build this Man of God a room. And, she said, "I perceive he is a holy man of God." They built him a room, and one day as he was laying in there, out of his office, he made something happen without, if I can say it this way, without an unction. As he was laying on the bed, Elisha said to his servant, "What does she need?" And the servant said, "I do not know." So he said, "Go get her." She stands at the door and he asks, "You want me to speak to the governor?" She says, "No, I dwell among my own people." He asks, "You want me to talk to them?" She responds with, "Nope, doing good." "You want me to do this?" "Nope, doing good." Remember that the Man of God initiated this? And then, finally the servant says, "She does not have a kid." To that Elisha says, "This time next year, thou shall have a kid." Note, he did that out of his office.

You are going to have to understand, the greater anointing on your life, whatever you start speaking, is going to come to pass quicker. That is why I made sure I watched Brother Hagin. I am a big one to kid. I like to kid, and I like to cut-up, but I am learning not to go quite as far as I use to. I am finding out that there are some things I just really, even kidding, do not need to say anymore, not from the place we are going, or to the place we are heading to.

33

So out of that office, Elisha initiated something. Scripture does not say, "The word of the lord came to him and said because this or that." He initiated; he said, "What does she need?" He did not have a word of knowledge; he did not have a clue about what she needed. He asked his servant, "Does she need to talk to the governor?" The answer was, "No!" Stop and think; there are things now that come out of your office. When people help you, when people are faithful to your ministry, the ministry of helps, and they are always connected, always willing to help, out of your office, you ought to be able to bless them if you desire to. And you will get some people who just do not understand. They will think, "Well they are always just friendly with these people." Well, that bunch over there, who is always willing to help out, understands the anointing on our lives and are doing their Pastors, best to help us get to where we need to get to. That woman never tried to buy anything spiritual from the Man of God; she saw that he was a holy man of God; she honored that office, and out of that office, that man initiated something.

Romans 11:29

For the gifts and calling of God are without repentance.

So I had told you that the Lord had asked about Romans 11:29, "For the gifts and calling of God are without repentance." He said that out of the two men he had talked to me about, "One of them would not judge himself in three areas he had asked him to do so. Then the other one, a man Gordon Lindsey went to 3 times to tell him, "You are called to this office, you know you are but do not teach, because when you teach, you bring harm to the body."

Brother Hagin would teach us, "Do not try to intrude into another man's office." If you are one, everybody will know it, and you will know it by the unction of the Holy Ghost. Just remember, you can drink diesel and live in a garage, but that does not make you a Mac truck. You can say you are one, but that does not make you one. It is the gifts and callings that make you one. (How do I know?)

And so the Lord sent these two and said the power began to flow. Then He said that because there were people just throwing so much money at them, it got one of them off. The other one got off because he wanted to start teaching and he was not a teacher; he was a prophet. And He said he was bringing harm to the body. He intruded into the wrong office. Do not intrude into the wrong office.

So if a greater degree of power is on you then the less room there is for error. That is why God was dealing with me. I remember when Brother Hagin said the Lord had dealt with him and had said to him, "I want you to quit having off-base crusades, go back into the local church." The Lord instructed him to start having Holy Ghost meetings. Brother Hagin told us, "I need some of you to come to these smaller meetings." He said, "I cannot move a bigger crowd, so we have to get out of the Civic Centers; I have to go back to smaller crowds where they will help move with me." I remember that he said it took him two years to get back into that flow, two years. We cannot be frustrated that it is taking so long, be thankful so that when you get there, you can stay. One of those ministers on the scene that I mentioned previously who refused to correct themselves, died at 38, of some heart trouble. The other one died at 42 or 43. He died in a car wreck. That is way too young; that is way, way, way too young.

2 Timothy 2:20-21

20But in a great house there are not only vessels of gold and of silver, but also of wood and of earth; and some to honour, and some to dishonour.

21If a man therefore purge himself from these, he shall be a vessel unto honour, sanctified, and meet for the master's use, and prepared unto every good work.

Here is something else that the Lord spoke to me that night in the cab of that truck. 2 Timothy 2:20 says: "But in a great house, there are not only vessels of gold and of silver, but also of wood, and of earth, some to honor, some to dishonor." Verse 21, "If a man therefore purge himself from these, he shall be a vessel unto honor." Then comes sanctified. Sanctified means, set apart. "Separate now unto me Barnabus and Saul," set apart, sanctified. So, "If a man therefore purge himself from these, he should be a vessel unto honor, sanctified, and meet for the Master's use, and prepared unto every good work." This is something the Lord asked me about. He said, "What does this mean?" Well, we have already figured out that if God asks us a question, more than likely we do not know the answer. So I said, "Lord, I do not know exactly what you want me to see, help me here." He talked to me first. He said, "You have got to understand, if the power was on you, and if there is any type of unsettledness then you might not make it."

I remember Brother Hagin telling us about all the stuff he went through. Out of that he wrote the book, 'Must Christians Suffer?'. In it he wrote about all the stuff he went through. He said, the Lord had told him, "I allowed you to go through a lot of this stuff, so that when you got to a certain office, you would be able to stay." You have to

36

prove your ministry. That is why he would not license and ordain a lot of them until after two years, to see if they were going to stick with what they said they were called.

So here he said, vessels. This is what the Lord asked me: He said, "What about the wood and earthen vessels?" He said, "All vessels will contain." Let us take a bottle of water. The bottle is basically a vessel. It is plastic. Although, they do not make it the same way they used to, that plastic. Used to be that you could take a milk jug, throw it outside somewhere like a trash pile or something like that. You could come back a year later and that thing would still be together. So they had to develop something that would degrade quicker in sunshine and heat so that it would go back to the Earth. Well, that is a vessel. So he said, "In a great house, there are many different types of vessels." Well, we can say that there are two different houses. There is an individual house, and then there is the corporate house that we are building for God, according to the book of Peter. So, he said, "There are many vessels in a house." Then he said, "There are wood, earth, gold, and silver." He said, "Did you notice, as you learned to develop, that wood or earthen vessels will always add a flavor to whatever they hold?" So he said, "I am teaching you some things so that as you are a carrier of the anointing, upon, that you will not add a flavor to it. A gold or silver vessel not only understands how to look better, but they hold things without ever adding to it."

2 Corinthians 10:12-13

12For we dare not make ourselves of the number, or compare ourselves with some that commend themselves: but they measuring themselves by themselves, and comparing themselves among themselves, are not wise.

13But we will not boast of things without our measure, but according to the measure of the rule which God hath distributed to us, a measure to reach even unto you.

In 2 Corinthians, chapter 10, verse 12 he starts off and he says, "For we dare not make ourselves of the number or compare ourselves with some who commend themselves, by themselves, measuring themselves, comparing themselves among themselves," That whole bunch is not wise. Verse 13: "But we will not boast of things without our measure." You have got to underline that or make a note of it: "We will not boast of things without our measure." If you recall previously we talked to you briefly about measures. Then Paul says, "We will not boast of things without our measure, but according to the measure of the rule," or line, string, "which God, hath distributed to us, a measure to reach even unto you."

I remember another instance Brother Hagin told us about where he was praying. And he said he realized he is doing something with his finger, so he opened his eyes, and he said he realized he made a little circle. Then he would make another larger circle, then he would make another even larger circle, and then he would make another circle. And so he said, "Lord I need an interpretation of that." And the Lord said, "These represent measures or phases." He said, "The first circle is about you leaving your church and start travelling." He said, "You will minister all over East and Southeast Texas." Then He said, "The next measure you will minister from the East boundary of Texas to the West boundary of Texas. Then the next measure will be from the East Coast to the West Coast. Then if you live long enough, the last circle will be from all over the entire world or go to all nations." Every circle represented increase, every one of them. So He says here, "We will not boast of things without our measure." And we know God sets the measure.

Genesis 2:15

And the LORD God took the man, and put him into the garden of Eden to dress it and to keep it.

I have shared this; I want to share it again. When God told Adam, he said, "you are responsible," Genesis 2:15, "to dress and keep the garden," keep it organized; that is what it meant. Alright, He said, "If any responsibility is ever given, there has to be authority to go with responsibility." What he was saying was, "I am giving you the responsibility of Eden, but then He is also going to have to give him authority. Here is also where Paul refers to when he says, "We will not boast of things without our measure."

We all know that there are different organizations that help oversee pastors and younger ministers. We personally oversee some young ministers coming up. Just like all of them, there are a lot of other ministers in the family of God. Listen to this; for me to look at somebody and say, "You know, if I was you, I think I would do this," is out of line. If I have not been given any responsibility, I have no right to touch what they are doing with my mouth. If I do, now I am judging. And everybody else will get to see me go through the exact same thing and see how I turn out. These are things I want you to understand are all in the area of measures.

There may be ministers who have submitted themselves and call us and say, "Hey, what do you think?" Then what they are doing is that they are putting themselves in a place that if something is going on, and we need to say then we speak from a place of authority, not from a place of being critical or judgmental. There will be some ministers doing some things where I can see what they are doing and I know that it will not be good, but still, I cannot speak to other ministers about that from the degree of being critical. If we are talking about having a guest speaker come then there are times we can sit down together and talk about instruction and things, but we are not jumping on people. But, to talk about somebody, "Well if I was you, I would do this." Remember, you do not qualify if you do not have any responsibility there.

So this is what some ministers started telling me. They would say, "You need to go to the East Coast. They would love you on the East Coast!" That is what they were telling me; this was a few years back. "You need to go to the East Coast!" But you have to understand, the only place God sent me on my measure, was from Oklahoma all the way to Old Mexico, all the way to Canada, and every state in the union west. And I would go to Chicago periodically because I was on a board there. That was it; that was all. And they would say, "Man you need to go to the Carolinas." "Man, you need to come to Florida! " and I would say, "Well, that is fine, but I am not called there." My measure at this time does not reach there. Do not go beyond your measure! If you go beyond your measure, you are going to have to pay for the trip like Jonah did with the ticket.

People say, "Well there is such need in Africa." Someday I will go to Africa. I will go; my wife and I will go; we will minister. There will be some things that will happen there. You see I had a vision one time of a man from Egypt that stood before me and said, "Come over and help us." We are going to go some day, but it is not time; my measure is not there. "Well there is such a need there." To that I respond, I cannot be moved by need; I am moved by the Holy Ghost. Then others insist, "You ought to come to the East Coast!" I respond with, "I will not go to the East Coast, not yet."

Paul said, "I will NOT go beyond my measure." This has to do with phases and rooms. I will NOT go beyond my measure. People come along, and they mean good, and they have right intentions, but they say, "Man, if I was you, I think I would start doing this." What they do not know is that if the Holy Ghost has not told me, I am not moving a peg. That is what people would tell Brother Hagin, "We ought to do this…" And they would get frustrated with him, because he would not say who was speaking at Camp Meetings, or who was doing such and such. He would say, "I am not saying until the Holy Ghost says. Then we will just make the call." He would say, "You want me to make the call? I would rather wait and hear from heaven, so that we do not have to backtrack and republish something!"

 So, what are you called to? What has God called you to do? What is the equipment on your life and to what degree of measure is on your life? Let the anointing within help develop character, so that as you increase in character and development and learn how to treat and work with people that are sometimes crazy. Used to be that the only way we knew how to deal with rude people was to bust them in the lip. That was it! We are learning to develop different ways of the anointing now!

2 Corinthians 10:12

For we dare not make ourselves of the number, or compare ourselves with some that commend themselves: but they measuring themselves by themselves, and comparing themselves among themselves, are not wise.

He said in verse 12: "We will not dare make ourselves of the number, or compare ourselves with some that commend themselves," that is very important, "through how they measure themselves." That is where the recommendation or commendation comes. They commend themselves. Let God promote you. "Well, if I could ever get on TV, I tell you, the world would see me!" The world is not ready to see you. You are not ready for television. People will say, "Boy if I could just do this, I could get exposed!" You better let God expose you. See that is why he says, "Let Him exalt you in due season." There is a season to these things. If you get out of the wrong season, you might end up over where it is 32 degrees with shorts and a tank top on. There are seasons!

You know Brother Hagin was a great success; he travelled all over the United States. I do not know that he went overseas a lot, but he held meetings; he stayed booked; he had to pray about where he went, and all. Not many really had heard about him until he got to be about 60 years old. And people would come and ask him, "Where have you been?" It was about 1983-84 when his ministry just like exploded. He had been out there since 1939 or 1938. Well, what happened was that he got to a place; he got to his fourth phase. And you can find it in the word; that is your harvest season.

Ezekiel 47:3

And when the man that had the line in his hand went forth eastward, he measured a thousand cubits, and he brought me through the waters; the waters were to the ankles.

Ezekiel, he stretched a line by an angel and there was water to the ankles to walk in; that is usually your first phase. He stretched another line, but it takes awhile to get across that ankle deep water. Then he stretched another one; there was water to the knees. That is a second phase and every phase will have rooms. Then he stretched another one; There is water to the loins. The last place he stretched it, there were waters to swim; that would be your harvest years. But you have got to live long enough to get there.

Some want huge churches and they want other things. If you go the way God says, many times it will seem like it takes way too long. And you can get them, bigger, if you will compromise what God told you to do. However, that is the wrong measure. God does not condemn anybody to a small church. We are not saying that. There will be increase; do not be frustrated; do not be upset if you have pastored somewhere for 15 years, and it just seems that it has not done what it is supposed to. Hang on. Stay with it because your harvest years are upon you.

We can all remember when we first started pastoring with 10 or 20 or 30. That is probably all really at that particular time we could handle. And then came the 50, and then a few more. No one should be frustrated over 50. Be thankful instead that God saw you fit to look over 50. "Well, I am not getting the great big meetings." Brother Hagin never was concerned about big meetings? He would go wherever the Lord said. Who cares about big meetings? I want the anointing to show up in every meeting I have. "Well if you get more people you will get more money." We are being moved by finances; wrong motive; wrong measure. If you go where God tells you to go, He will supply your needs. He is obligated to do it!

2 Corinthians 10:12

For we dare not make ourselves of the number, or compare ourselves

with some that commend themselves: but they measuring themselves by themselves, and comparing themselves among themselves, are not wise.

So he said, "We dare not make ourselves a number, or compare ourselves with some that commend themselves." Do not commend yourself; let God do it. "But they measure themselves by themselves." Let us not forget that there are people, who use the wrong measuring stick. They will measure their success by how many they have. I measure my success by if I am still doing the word that God gave me. That is success; that is how we measure.

Ezekiel 47:3

And when the man that had the line in his hand went forth eastward, he measured a thousand cubits, and he brought me through the waters; the waters were to the ankles.

Ezekiel 47:3 says, "And when the man had the line in his hand, went forth Eastward, he measured a thousand cubits." We can all agree this is a form of measurement. "He measured a thousand cubits, and he brought me through the waters. The waters were to the ankles." Do not be frustrated. Remember Job 8:7 says not to despise the small things. That means do not become disdained, do not look down on small beginnings. He said do not despise when everything is still small. Do not view small beginnings as not important. If you do not see it as small or disdained, or despaired it will not stay small. If we stay with the plan of God, we are going to get out of ankle deep water. Right now we are glad to be in the ankle deep water, because we are at least in the water. It is good to recognize, however, that it is going to take a

44

while to get across this ankle deep water. But, once I get to the other side of it, what is next? Knee deep. Now there is a greater flow, a greater measure, a greater anointing. Because the character has come with me through the ankle deep, now I can walk in a greater anointing. For me to run through the ankle deep water to get to the knee deep, I might miss some steps or some things I should have gone through to help develop some things.

Ezekiel 47:4-5

4Again he measured a thousand, and brought me through the waters; the waters were to the knees. Again he measured a thousand, and brought me through; the waters were to the loins.

5Afterward he measured a thousand; and it was a river that I could not pass over: for the waters were risen, waters to swim in, a river that could not be passed over.

So he says here, "Again, he measured a thousand; he brought me through the waters. The waters were to the knees, he measured a thousand, he brought me through the water to the loins." Verse 5, "Afterward he measured a thousand and it was a RIVER that I could not pass over, for the waters were risen, waters to swim in." And those are what we can call the harvest years; Waters to swim in is a full flow. It took a time to get there, measure.

A few years ago a person said, "We want you to go to Peru with us." I said, at that time, "I do not go to Peru. I stay... I go from Oklahoma to Texas and all the way to Canada and every state in the Union West. That is basically where I go and I do go to Chicago." And I said, "That is really it, but I do not go out that far yet." And so I began to pray about it, and the Lord said, "I want you to go because," he said, "if you will go, you are going to go into another room." So I said, "Yes sir, I will go." So I told them I would go, and we went. We went down to some people that have a bible school there and they were celebrating 25 years of connecting with Rhema.

I travelled with, Dr. Dufresne. When it was his time to speak, he said, "I want you to speak in my place." And I said, "Yes, Sir!" So I was ministering and when I got through he said, "I see you did not get through." He said, "Speak in my place tonight." So I did, and when I got through, when I was up front he got up, and came walking towards me. As I was standing, he said, "Are you through?" and I said, "Yes sir." When I said that, he slapped me; he slapped me hard and he said, "You now go into your next room." He did not know. So after awhile I began to pray, and I said, "God I want to know something; what is in this room?" He said, "In this room, is a room of the miraculous. There are miracles in this room."

Every phase will have rooms. If I was to come to your house, and I was to come into the front room, in the front room there could be a couch, a recliner, a coffee table; there could be some other things; there could be some entertainment centers, things like that; that is a room in that house, but that is not all the rooms in that house. So as soon as I leave the front room and I got to the kitchen I am in the same house, but now I am in another room, and everything in this room is completely different. There is all new equipment here. Now I have to learn to operate or work with every piece of equipment that is in this room.

See this is where sometimes people struggle. They will go into another phase, but then in that phase there is also usually several rooms in a phase. That is why with Brother Hagin, in certain phases, the Lord would say, "Okay, quit going to having all faith crusades. Immediately start having Holy Ghost meetings." He was still in his 4ᵗʰ phase but he had gone into another room. The Lord would direct him like this. And that is sometimes because it is a shift; it is a change. Sometimes people do not go because it is new, because it takes a year or two to learn to work with this equipment. We are creatures of habit. And if the Lord tells us to pastor, and we are pastoring, and we are in a certain phase in pastoring, just because you go to another phase does not mean you leave the office you stand in. There are different degrees of the same office. And the Lord will say, "This year I want you to go after this through the local church." And you might emphasize this year, it is soul winning. Next year all of a sudden the Lord might say, "This year, lets minister to all of those that are in the family." You have got to pay attention to what room he has lead you into and work with every piece of equipment.

1 Corinthians 12:28

And God hath set some in the church, first apostles, secondarily prophets, thirdly teachers, after that miracles, then gifts of healings, helps, governments, diversities of tongues.

So when we went to Peru, he said, "You have now gone into another room." And I said, "What is in this room?" and he took me, and that is what I talked to many of you about 1 Corinthians 12:28, miracles. It is not the same as working in miracles as one of the gifts. All of them listed in verse 28 are all ministry offices, every one of them. There are those that will have miracles upon them as a ministry gift. Not to say that it will not flow through others. Because, let us not forget, the gifts of the spirit are for the whole church.

1 Corinthians 16:9

For a great door and effectual is opened unto me, and there are many adversaries.

1 Corinthians 16:9 states, "For a great door and effectual is open unto me, but there are many adversaries." The Amplified says, "For a wide door of opportunity for effectual service has opened to me... there a great and promising one,", "and there are many adversaries." What is an open door to you and I? That could be another phase that could be a room.

Remember that song we used to sing? "Beyond the open door is a new and fresh anointing." That is scriptural you know. It is the same Holy Ghost, but now it is a different measure. We learn to work with the Holy Ghost, or the anointing in our office, a certain place. Then, if it shifts, many times that is where we struggle. "Beyond the open door is a new and fresh anointing. Step on through the door; hear the spirit calling." That is how we go, "Hear the spirit calling you to go. Walk on through the door, for the Lord will go before you, into a greater power than you have ever known before." That is a new place! That is a new room or a new phase, that is a new anointing, same Holy Ghost, but now there is increase.

But what is there, there at the door, for you to step through? According to 1 Corinthians 16:9, "many adversaries." Usually right when you are getting ready to go into another phase or room, all hell breaks out and you are like, "Dear God what is going on?" Probably, there is promotion and the devil knows if he can get you so discouraged, you will not step through that door. Because you are so busy trying to put out all the fires. These things are designed as distractions.

Luke 11:24-27

48

24When the unclean spirit is gone out of a man, he walketh through dry places, seeking rest; and finding none, he saith, I will return unto my house whence I came out.

25And when he cometh, he findeth it swept and garnished.

26Then goeth he, and taketh to him seven other spirits more wicked than himself; and they enter in, and dwell there: and the last state of that man is worse than the first.

27And it came to pass, as he spake these things, a certain woman of the company lifted up her voice, and said unto him, Blessed is the womb that bare thee, and the paps which thou hast sucked.

Luke 11: 24 says, "When the unclean spirit is gone out of a man, he walketh through dry places seeking rest and finding none he saith I will return to my house whence I came out. And when he cometh, he findeth it swept and garnished. He goeth, take it with him, seven other spirits more wicked than himself and they enter in, and dwell there and the last state of the man is worse than the first." So, he is teaching a lesson here on dealing with the devil and how the devil gets in. Verse 27 continues, "And it came to pass, as he spake these things, a certain woman of the company lifted up her voice and said unto him, blessed is the womb that bear thee, and paps which thou hast sucked." Wrong emphasis. He had just taught a solid bible lesson on how the devil gets in and how he will try to bring other spirits with him, and all this woman got out of the message was, "Dear God, who's your mama?"

Luke 11:28

But he said, Yea rather, blessed are they that hear the word of God, and keep it.

49

Wrong emphasis. Wrong emphasis. Jesus does not even acknowledge what she says; look what he does. Verse 28, "But he said, yea rather blessed are they that hear the word of God, and keep it." He brought the focus back to where it needed to be. Stay focused; do not let things pull your attention; do not let things have the wrong emphasis. Years ago, I remember a minister said, and I could have even said it too at one time when I was ignorant, but you know, I am not a genius yet, but I am getting there, I have got somebody in me that knows everything. I am borderline genius. But you know, this one minister said, "Dear God I would have the time of my life in ministry if it just were not for people." Well, unfortunately you cannot have a ministry without people. People are what helps do the ministry, makes the ministry. So, therefore, "Wrong emphasis."

Now listen to this one. Brother Hagin made this statement, he said the Lord Jesus told him, "You have got to understand, I called you to the office of a prophet. I told you to start Rhema." Meaning, "Do not EVER let Rhema take priority over what I have called you to." Rhema would need money every month and different things, but he said, "If you get it out of spec, it is going to create problems for you." You cannot let things distract you from what you are called. Always flow in your measure.

Galatians 2:7

But contrariwise, when they saw that the gospel of the uncircumcision was committed unto me, as the gospel of the circumcision was unto Peter;

Galatians 2:7 says, "But counter wise when they saw that the gospel of the uncircumcision was committed unto me," Paul writes, "And the gospel of the circumcision was unto Peter." He knew his measure.

After Peru and after I got home, the Lord said, "Okay, I now want you to start going from East Coast to West Coast." And it has now begun to happen. And now we go to the East Coast; we go to the West Coast. Well, I have got to live long enough to get from the East Coast to the West Coast to around the world. These things are steps, there are procedures, there are measures, and it will apply to every office.

2 Corinthians 10:13 (NLT)

We will not boast about things done outside our area of authority. We will boast only about what has happened within the boundaries of the work God has given us, which includes our working with you.

So Paul knew exactly where he was called to be. 2 Corinthians 10:13 out of the NLT says, "We will not boast about things done outside our area of authority. We will boast about things within the boundaries of the work God has given to us," not outside our area of authority.

Luke 19:17

And he said unto him, Well, thou good servant: because thou hast been faithful in a very little, have thou authority over ten cities.

Luke 19:17 says, "And he said unto him, well thou good servant, because thou has been faithful." Remember faithfulness is always the key, "because thou has been faithful, in a very little, have thou authority over ten cities." When you and I got saved or take born again believers, do they have the authority given to them that is granted by the name of Jesus? We can all agree on yes. That cannot increase. What can increase is the revelation of what is in that authority. But all that is in that name is given to everybody when they are born again. So here, he cannot be talking about the name of Jesus. Because now he is saying your area of authority is going to increase. This has to do with measure. Your realm of influence will grow as you are found faithful and you go through every measure. So he said, "You can now have authority over," how many cities? "10 Cities."

2 Corinthians 13:5

Examine yourselves, whether ye be in the faith; *word* **prove your own selves. Know ye not your own selves, how that Jesus Christ is (in) you, except ye be reprobates?**

When we look at 2 Corinthians 13:5, Paul does not say to examine your wife because God knows she needs help nor to examine your husband because God knows he needs help. No it does not say that. It does not say any of that. What it does say is to examine yourself. It says to examine myself, "Whether I be in the faith."

Romans 10:17

So then faith cometh by hearing, and hearing by the word of God.

Romans 10:17 says, "So then faith cometh by hearing," and whatever part of the word I heard that I believe will always qualify as faith. That is why people can be in a service, and you can preach a message about healing and some will believe what they hear, and they will get healed. There will be others that will hear the message, but they will not believe it or to whatever degree they hear or believe it, is only the part of degree they have, right? So he says in 2 Corinthians 13:5, "Examine yourself whether you be in faith."

Galatians 2:7

But contrariwise, when they saw that the gospel of the uncircumcision was committed unto me, as the gospel of the circumcision was unto Peter;

Let us look back to Galatians 2:7. We read that God told Paul to go to the uncircumcisioned, which are the Gentiles. Now you remember, he tried to preach to the Jews; he finally got so frustrated he said, "I am going back to the gentiles." He said, "I will tell you what, you folk are eating me up!" He was in the wrong measure. So he finally went back to the gentiles, and then he wrote about it and said, "I found my place, I found where I belong."

Now here is the deal, God told him in 2 Corinthians 12, when he was caught up to the 3rd heaven, when he heard words that were unlawful for man such as Paul to hear, " Let a man examine himself." Then he would come back and write a lot of our New Testaments in the epistles. Well, God gave him a specific word to go minister out of his measure.

So here he wrote and he said, "Let a man examine himself." This is what I wrote in my bible; this is how God taught me; He said, "For my age," talking to me, "For my age, am I about where I need to be to finish my course? For my age, am I in about the right phase of ministry? For My age, am I where I about need to be to completely finish?" I have to examine myself." You know, I would like to stay home with my wife and my kids and my grandbabies. However, I do not pastor, I co-pastor with her. I am not a pastor any more. So the word God gave me was to travel, "Go!" So I have to constantly examine myself to see if I am still in the word, the faith that God gave me.

Romans 13:23

And he that doubteth is damned if he eat, because he eateth not of faith: for whatsoever is not of faith is sin.

Int!

And if we look at Romans 14:23 we see that, "Whatsoever is not of faith is sin." I have used the following demonstration many times before. Let us say the Lord told me to give someone $50. So I look in my wallet, and all I have is $100. So I say, "Well I do not want to give him $50, I want to give him $30." The word was 50. Can I give him $30? Yes. Can I attach any FAITH to that word? NO! Why? The word was $50. I am talking about the God kind of faith.

When people get frustrated and offended at a church, or a minister gets tired of preaching and decides, "I am going to go back to selling cars," or somebody gets offended at a church although God said, "That is your home church," and they get frustrated, and they leave that church and go somewhere else, do you know, they can never attend another church by faith? I am talking about the God kind of faith and God gave them a certain word. You can have faith in other things, but remember Jesus said the only kind of way to have the God kind of faith is to have the God kind of word. So if God said, "This is your home church." And they get offended and they leave, and God did not say, "Go." The word was for the church they attend and they go over to Hubba-ubba-Bubba's church. I think we can agree that they can attend Hubba-ubba-Bubba's church, but they cannot go over there by faith because they do not have a God kind of word so, you cannot have the God kind of faith. I could stay home, but I cannot stay home by faith because I do not have a God word to stay home. I can travel by faith therefore I can please God.

X Awesome!

Alright, so, "Examine ourselves to see whether or not we are in the faith." This is what I wrote. "Test yourselves to make sure you are

54

solid in faith. Do not drift along taking everything for granted." Give yourselves a regular checkup. Ask yourself, "How am I doing where I am to flow? Am I on schedule for my age; am I about right? Am I in the right phase for this time? Am I in the right room?" I want to be like Paul where he said in 2 Timothy 4:7, "I have kept the faith. I have kept the Word, I have finished my course."

I remember in 1999, we were in a meeting with Brother Hagin. He was praying in tongues and the power of God was on him; finally he said, "Get me a chair." He was praying and then he started praying in tongues and said, "and now I enter into the last room. The final room of my 4th phase." But then as he prayed in tongues and started laughing like he did often, he said, "I am not going to die next week. I am not going to die next month, not going to die next year, not going to die next year." And we figured it up, and it went right up to 2003, because this is what he said, "An extension has been put on to the room." We were in that meeting; we have still have the tape. He said, "An extension was put on the room." We did not know there was an exit room. It is like the green room when you come to speak; it is where you get ready to speak; there is a place to go when you get ready to leave.

So, for my age, am I about right? For my age, am I about where I need to be to finish my course? I know we are promised 120 years, I know we are. But folks, I will be honest with you, I am not going to travel hard and fast when I am 70 like I do right now. I will still travel, I will still be wealthy and healthy should Jesus tarry. But, we are going to have more and more meetings, the older I get; we are going to have more and more meetings at the house. That is how the Lord directed me; that is why we are constructing a new building, because we are going to have more and more meetings there in Pawnee. But, I will go and I will still travel at 70, I will still travel at 75 should Jesus tarry, but I am not going to go like I am going now. For my age, am I about on course? Can I finish, Lord, the race that you have for me from where I am right now? We are interested in these things, Glory to God. And if we ministers can get it, then we can teach our ministry of helps because there are rooms and phases there too. Thank God for the Holy Ghost. We are going to drink from the well, and we are going to learn to flow with the river in greater measures. Glory! We are increasing in the river, in the anointing, in our measures.

Chapter 3: Your Full Supply

We read in Brother Hagin's book *Understanding the Anointing* on page 139, he talked about "The Anointing Within." You can never find scripture anyplace that will verify that the anointing within will ever increase. However the anointing within will do several things; it will teach you; it will train you. He has there to lead and guide you, but also he has there to help develop character. Let us go back to the night I was in the cab of my truck and the presence of God came in. He began to talk to me at about 1:00 a.m. out on I-40. That time He talked to me and said, "You been bother…bugging me." That is how he said it to me, "Bugging me about an increase of the power." He said, "I am not holding anything back because I do not love you or I do not want you to have it, but," he said, "You have got to come up by the anointing within, so that when the anointing upon comes up, the anointing within has brought you up to a place so that your character will match what you are flowing in."

He talked to me about different ministers God had sent Brother Hagin to talk to one of them about three things. The Power of God was flowing through him but because people were revering and idolizing him, it started to get to him. One time he called a fellow minister up in the middle of the night, 2AM, not to tell him, "Thank you for doing a good job." No, he called him up at 2AM, woke him up, and said to him, "I just wanted you to know I got a new wing to my tent and it added 6,000 more people, and my tent now seats 26,000." The other minister had one that seated 22,000. He just called him up in the middle of the night to let him know his tent was bigger than his. If you ask me, that was really not in the love of God. However, God was using him mightily. We needed him longer than 38, though. He left planet Earth at thirty-eight years: Thirty-eight years of age. We needed that ministry to go on over into his seventies and eighties; we needed him on Earth. And then there was another minister he left early as well. He left at forty.

Romans 11:29

For the gifts and calling of God are without repentance.

God talked to me about letting the anointing within develop the character. He said, "Romans 11:29 says that the gifts and callings of God are irrevocable, cannot be taken back, cannot change." So he said, "Once the power of God flows to a certain degree, I cannot never pull that back. If you allow people to pull you off, or their influence pulls you off, or money starts pulling you off, I cannot pull the power back because it is irrevocable, cannot be changed, cannot be taken back." So he said, "As soon as that starts happening, the power is no longer a blessing to you in your life; the power is now immediately working against you, and it will cause your life to be short."

So we want to know about these things. Someone asked me recently what I have been preaching about these days and I said that I have been talking about rooms; "I am talking about phases and rooms," I said. I mentioned to this one person that whom we had gone to school under, Brother Hagin, had talked about it. I was surprised to hear that he did not know. He said, "What is a phase? What is a room?"

Well dear God, if Jesus appeared to Brother Hagin, and told him, "Many of my ministers live and die and never get into the first phase," then this must be something I ought to pay attention to. I am married to a pretty woman. I do not want to leave early; somebody else will have her. I have got a course to finish; I have got a race to run. I want to be like the apostle Paul and I want to say I finished my course; I kept the faith, henceforth there is laid up for me a crown of righteousness. But, you have got to get to every phase and every room to finish completely, not be finished but to finish.

We said that the anointing upon could absolutely be increased. We also said that for the anointing within we could not find scripture saying that it will increase but that the revelation of what that anointing will bring you, will develop you, teach you, and train you, leading to character development. It is more than likely that you do not deal with people the same way you did when you first started out in the ministry. You have greater understanding. There is a greater anointing; there is more compassion about some things. On the other hand, we can see some things quicker now because we have been down that road before.

1 Kings 19:16

And Jehu the son of Nimshi shalt thou anoint to be king over Israel: and Elisha the son of Shaphat of Abelmeholah shalt thou anoint to be prophet in thy room.

1 Kings 19:16 says, "And Jehu the son of Nimshi shalt thou anoint to be king over Israel. And Elisha the son of Shaphat of Abelmeholah

59

shalt thou anoint to be prophet in thy room." It says that Elisha, the son of Shaphat, "shalt thou anoint to be prophet in thy room." Now my question is this, how come God is having Elijah invite Elisha into his room? We have been over quite a bit about phases and rooms. And, we talked about 2 Corinthians 10: 12 & 13 where Paul says, "I never went beyond my measure." We have gone over how brother Hagin had taught to never intrude into another man's office. The NLT says it a little differently, "I never went beyond my area of authority." We also talked about Luke 19:17, "Have thou now authority over 10 cities, because you been found faithful."

The authority or your realm of influence will get broader with the maturing of the things of the spirits you get into. Let us be glad that when we first started out we only got about 5 folks because, let us face it, some of the stuff we preached, thank God back then we did not record everything, because it was not that good; maybe we thought it was, but it was not that great. However, it was all we had and we were doing the best we could. But, as we grow and we mature, we preach better; we minister better. You know, it is amazing that there is no instruction, when you have a child, on how to raise a kid. You just do the best you can with the first one; then have another one and do better. Then, at about time you get through with 4 or 5 or however many you have, you are an expert! And by the time they are all grown and left, you know how to raise kids!

Well, in the same way, for some of these things we do not really have an instruction manual. But God will put a man or a woman of God into your life and He will allow them to invite you or me into their room, and there is a reason for it, because we do not know how all of this functions. I would go to Brother Hagin's meetings and I would sit, and sometimes when he was praying for people I would know others would bow their head, but I would always watch him. I was not trying to be disrespectful, I had my eyes open and I would watch him like a hawk. You see I needed to know how he ministered to some. I needed to know what the Holy Ghost would do, because God had sent my wife and me to Rhema, If he sent me to Rhema, then he sent me there to learn some stuff. And if God sends you to a local church, that pastor has something to impart into you to get the ministry that God called you to, out of you. However, if you are flighty, or all around crazy, they cannot ever get you long enough to develop you.

So he says here that he invited him. "Thou shall anoint Elisha to be prophet in thy room." Some translations say, "in thy stead"; some translations say, "in thy place." In 2 Kings where they come up to the river, there are several things here I want you to please understand, Elijah said to Elisha, "Tarry you here while I go on." He responded with, "Nay my Lord, I have been washing your hands and taking care of you for 15 years." You have got to catch these things: And they went a little further and he said, "Well, why do not you just wait here and I will go on a little further." There are some times God wants to know right before it is time for you to get into some things if you are really serious and you are going to prove out good and you are going to stay with it. Again, Elijah said, "You wait right here." Elisha said, "Nay my Lord, I have been with you, I have stayed with you, I am still going to be with you." So they finally got up to the brook, and the Man of God took his mantle and he smote the water and they walked across on dry ground. Then he said, "Before I go, if you see me, what do you want?" To that Elisha said, "I want a double portion." Elijah said, "If you see me you can have it. He saw something on his Man of God, on his pastor, on his spiritual Father, and he said, "Whatever is on you I want." ⭐

Luke 6:40

matture

The disciple is not above his master: but every one that is perfect shall be as his master.

Many times transfers come through environment, association, and influence. Luke 6:40 says that the people will never rise above the master. And however your master sees something, then that is how you are going to end up seeing it. So follow those that have an eye to see into the realm of the spirit, and to know the Holy Ghost.

So they got to the other side and Elisha screamed and said, "Alas my master! Alas." When he hollered he said, "If you see me when I am gone, you can have it." There, I guess maybe they were walking side by side, I do not know if he walked beside him or a little behind him but they are walking. The scripture says, that a fiery chariot busts between the two of them. I do not know if Elisha fell because of the presence of God but I think maybe he did because of the manifestation of power. But when he gathered himself up, the bible seems to tell us that he looked undoubtedly, Elijah is already on his way up and he hollered and said, "ALAS MY MASTER ALAS!!!!!" In other words, "I see, I get it!"

I picture it this way; this is how the Lord helped me understand: Elijah at that time is headed up in the fiery chariot. He takes off his mantle, which represented his office, and throws it back to the Earth. Elisha sees it coming down takes his off, tears it up, in other words, I have served faithfully in the ministry of helps; I have served faithfully in the things God has called me to. And he took it, and he threw it off! And

62

he walked over and he picked up a new place where he has going to walk now! He put that on, and he went back to the creek. He took the mantle and he smote the waters. How did he know to smote the water? He hung out with somebody that had walked with the Holy Ghost enough to know the voice of the Holy Ghost, that is how. And he took that mantle and he smote the waters. He said, "Where be the Lord God of Elijah?" The waters opened up and he walked across. Run with those that know the moving of the Holy Ghost!

2 Kings 2:2

And Elijah said unto Elisha, Tarry here, I pray thee; for the LORD hath sent me to Bethel. And Elisha said unto him, As the LORD liveth, and as thy soul liveth, I will not leave thee. So they went down to Bethel.

2 Kings, chapter 2 says, "And Elijah said unto Elisha, 'tarry here I pray thee. For the Lord has sent me to Bethel," Elisha said, "As the Lord thy God liveth, and as I so liveth, I will not leave you." You have got to understand that whomever God told you to hook up to, do not you let any kind of offense drive you away. If God gave you a mentor, you have got to remember, there are several people you need in your life. You need a pastor, you need a spiritual Father, and you need a Timothy.

Many times I have seen God send somebody to help a pastor and I see the hand of God on them but just because you are called does not mean you are ready. The call is there, but now we have got to develop some things; we have got to get some things out of you.

2 Kings 2:4-6

4 And Elijah said unto him, Elisha, tarry here, I pray thee; for the LORD hath sent me to Jericho. And he said, As the LORD liveth, and as thy soul liveth, I will not leave thee. So they came to Jericho.

5And the sons of the prophets that were at Jericho came to Elisha, and said unto him, Knowest thou that the LORD will take away thy master from thy head today? And he answered, Yea, I know it; hold ye your peace.

6And Elijah said unto him, Tarry, I pray thee, here; for the LORD hath sent me to Jordan. And he said, As the LORD liveth, and as thy soul liveth, I will not leave thee. And they two went on.

So then he said, "I will not leave." Elisha said, under Elijah. Verse 4, "Tarry here," he said. "No sir," being kind about it. "As the Lord thy God liveth, as I shall liveth, I will not leave you. So they come to Jericho. Son of the prophet said some things; Elijah said unto him, verse 6, "Tarry, I pray thee here, for the Lord has sent me to Jordan." He said, "As the Lord thy God liveth, as I shall liveth I will not leave you."

You should promise yourself, "I am not leaving. I am not leaving. I am not leaving. I am not leaving my office, and I am not leaving my man or woman of God that God told me to hook up with. I am not leaving! I am not leaving! I am not leaving!" I said, "I am not leaving!" My pastor talked about that. I am not leaving! God told me to be here and God and I are on talking terms. If it is time for me to go, He will tell me, otherwise I am not going anywhere. I am staying put because there is a race to be run and there are some things I am fixing to receive, glory to God!

2 Kings 2:8-9

8And Elijah took his mantle, and wrapped it together, and smote the waters, and they were divided hither and thither, so that they two went over on dry ground.

9And it came to pass, when they were gone over, that Elijah said unto Elisha, Ask what I shall do for thee, before I be taken away from thee. And Elisha said, I pray thee, let a double portion of thy spirit be upon me.

So he said, "I ain't going nowhere, sir," kind, respectfully. Verse 8, it says here, "And Elisha took his mantle, and wrapped it together, smote the waters, they were divided thither and hither, so they went across on dry ground. It came to pass when they were going over, Elijah said unto Elisha, "Ask what I should do for thee before I would be taken away from thee." And Elisha said, "I pray let a double portion of thy spirit be upon me." Glory to God! I do not know how much of Brother Hagin's anointing I got, but I am telling you, I stayed close. I read books. I listen to tapes. I hung out with him, and attended a lot of the meetings. And you can still get some impartation off of the printed page and off of the teaching CDs.

A lot of time people will think, "Well I wonder who is going to get his mantle." I remember when Smith Wigglesworth left planet Earth, and Brother Hagin said, all of them was discussing it in a Pentecostal service, "I wonder who is going to get Smith Wigglesworth's anointing." Brother Hagin said, "It do not come that way. It comes by association, influence and environment. Everybody that listened to him, followed him closely, will all get some of it, Glory to God!" And as my pastor said, "Do not be deceived." In other words, if God told you to hook up with a man of God, there is a reason for it. Do not you leave too soon. Do not you let the devil drag you off to somewhere else. Now I am not saying that who he is taking you to is not a pastor. All I am saying is that you are careful they can flow with the Holy Ghost. I want to go somewhere where it is not just the word, but it' also a move of the Holy Ghost, glory to God! Be careful. A lot of pastors will say the Holy Ghost cannot interrupt because they've got their own little program! What they aught to do is let the Holy Ghost direct the service, glory to God!!!

2 Kings 2:10-11

10And he said, Thou hast asked a hard thing: nevertheless, if thou see me when I am taken from thee, it shall be so unto thee; but if not, it shall not be so.

11And it came to pass, as they still went on, and talked, that, behold, there appeared a chariot of fire, and horses of fire, and parted them both asunder; and Elijah went up by a whirlwind into heaven.

"Let a double portion of thy spirit be upon me!" So he says, "Thou ask a hard thing. Nevertheless, if thou see me when I am taken from thee, it shall be so unto thee; but if not," sorry, no. But if you see me, "And it came to pass as they still went on and talked, and behold there appeared a chariot of fire, horses of fire, parted them both asunder, and Elijah went up in a whirlwind." It parted them both asunder. It ran between them. They were just walking, talking, and the presence of God, a fiery chariot, they are walking and it goes between them, parts them asunder. When he finally comes to, he is up there and then the mantle happens.

2 Kings 6:1-2

1And the sons of the prophets said unto Elisha, Behold now, the place where we dwell with thee is too strait for us.

2Let us go, we pray thee, unto Jordan, and take thence every man a beam, and let us make us a place there, where we may dwell. And he answered, Go ye.

2 Kings Chapter 6, verse 1 says, "And the sons of the Prophet said unto Elijah, 'behold now the place where we dwell with thee is too straight for us. Let us go we pray thee unto Jordan and take thee, thence every man a beam, let us make us a place there where we may dwell' and he answered and said, 'it will be fine." Under the old covenant they needed a prophet, priest or king to talk to God for them. But under the new covenant, you and I can talk to God every day, every hour of the day, every minute of the day. You and I have the same Holy Ghost on the inside of us to lead and guide us. But, there is still the office of the prophet. However, we are not lead by the prophets. We are lead by the Holy Ghost. We are lead by the spirit of God! I believe with all of my heart.

I remember Brother Hagin said some things. Every time he would get over in the spirit, and he would get way over, he would say, "Lord God, what is that? What is that? What is that? I do not understand, what is that?" and he would say, "Oh my, my, my!" He would begin to get concerned, and he would come back. And then he would get in another meeting and get way over in the spirit again and say, "Oh my God! Oh my God!" Not speaking negatively, but in respect and reverence. "Oh my God! Oh my God!" He would say, "Lord every time I see that, every time..." Finally he began to explain to us what he was seeing. He was seeing a great outpouring of the Holy Ghost; he was seeing a move of the spirit of God; he was seeing all the gifts of the spirit in manifestation; he was seeing all the previous revivals now coming together, Glory to God! he would say. "I do not know if I will live long enough to see it, but it will all come to pass! It will all come to pass; it will all come to pass!

2 Kings 6:2-3

2Let us go, we pray thee, unto Jordan, and take thence every man a beam, and let us make us a place there, where we may dwell. And he answered, Go ye.

3And one said, Be content, I pray thee, and go with thy servants. And he answered, I will go.

2 Kings 6:2 says, "Let us go, we pray thee, unto Jordan, and take thence every man a beam, and let us make us a place there, where that we may dwell. And he answered," and he said, "Go ye." Verse 3, "And one said,' would you mind, would it be okay, if you can go with us?" When you are getting ready to build something, whether it is a ministry, whether it is a life, it is important whom you ask to go with you. And he said to him, he said, "Would it be okay if we go get a beam because we are out of room over here?" And he said, "It'd be fine." Then he said, "Would it be alright sir, since we are going, would you go with us?" You do not go to your pastor for direction; you go to the Holy Ghost. But you go to your Pastor to confirm some things that the Holy Ghost is telling you. Because if you will receive the pastor through the office of a pastor, how many of you know, you are going to get the benefit of the office of a shepherd? They said, "If you would, would you please go with us? Would you mind going with us?" He

said, "No, no, would not mind a bit." Glory to God, would not mind a bit.

2 Kings 6:4-7

4So he went with them. And when they came to Jordan, they cut down wood.

5But as one was felling a beam, the axe head fell into the water: and he cried, and said, Alas, master! for it was borrowed.

6And the man of God said, Where fell it? And he shewed him the place. And he cut down a stick, and cast it in thither; and the iron did swim.

7Therefore said he, Take it up to thee. And he put out his hand, and took it.

Verse 4, "So he went with them and when they came to Jordan they were cutting down wood. But as one was falling the beam, the axe head fell into the water. He cried and said 'alas my master, for it was borrowed.' And the man of God said, 'show me where it fell.'" Now we have heard this taught before. The young man said, "Alas my master it was borrowed." That axe was a tool or a piece of equipment that he used in the ministry and he lost it. Well, when you have invited your pastors, when you have invited your man of God to go with you to build something, even though maybe something was lost, that maybe you do not know how to flow with, certain things can help you; they can teach you; And, they can help recover some things. So he said, "Show me. Show me where it fell. He showed him the place and he cut down a stick and cast it in thither, and the iron got up and swam." Then he said, "Take it up. He took it, he put out his hand and he took it up." He had lost a piece of equipment that he needed for the

69

ministry. And what did he do? He asked his man of God to help him recover it.

1 Corinthians 11:28-29

28 But let a man examine himself, and so let him eat of that bread, and drink of that cup.

29 For he that eateth and drinketh unworthily, eateth and drinketh damnation to himself, not discerning the Lord's body.

1 Corinthians 11:28-29 says, "Let a man examine himself, so let him eat of that bread and drink of that cup. For he that eateth and drinketh unworthily eateth and drinketh damnation to himself." Here is what I am going after: "Not discerning the Lord's body." Now we have made a note of this. I need to examine my flow to the Body of Christ. I need to examine my flow to the Body of Christ. We all have a flow to the body. But, would you agree with me, through my flow, through your flow, there will be a flow of God, a thing of supply that willl help the Body of Christ. So, I might need to understand, examine, if God calls me to do a very specific thing, then I need to examine that is my flow to the Body of Christ. And if I examine that, there are some benefits for it.

Chapter 4: Art of Following

1 Kings 19:16

And Jehu the son of Nimshi shalt thou anoint to be king over Israel: and Elisha the son of Shaphat of Abelmeholah shalt thou anoint to be prophet in thy room.

In 1 Kings Chapter 19, verse 16, the Lord talks to the prophet Elijah and he tells him to go do some things, and then he says, "And go find Elisha, the son of Shaphat," and he said, "thou shall anoint him to be prophet in thy room." Now I know some bibles say, "To be prophet in thy place; To be prophet in thy stead." But also, the Lord told Elijah to invite Elisha into his room. And when he invited him into his room, he was going to teach him, demonstrate to him the flow of the Holy Ghost. It is always important to have someone that we are connected to. You know, Jesus, as soon as he got here and started his ministry, immediately began to choose people that he could impart things into. You know, Moses, he had Joshua. Elijah had Elisha. And then, the list just goes on. Paul had a Timothy. Jesus had his disciples. So, we can see patterns many times from the scripture, and these are things that will be very important to us.

In Luke Chapter 6 it will talk about, "Can the blind lead the blind?" And we know they cannot, because Jesus said that they would both fall into the ditch. But then he said, "The pupil, the student, will never be

71

above his Master," the subject here then is leadership. And he said, "If you see something a certain way, it is because whoever you are submitting to sees it that way." And it will talk about a moat, and it will talk about a beam, but the subject has to do with leadership. That is why we are hooked up with people that see and know more things of the spirit and by the spirit than we know. They can help expand our vision.

So he invited Elisha into his room. Well, we know Jesus appeared to Brother Hagin, and if you have read, his book, *Understanding the Anointing*, Jesus appeared to Brother Hagin and he said, "You are just now entering into the first phase of your ministry." And Brother Hagin said, "I know that cannot be right." He said, "Dear God I have been preaching for fifteen years! That cannot be right!" And then He said, Jesus said, "Many of my servants live and die and never get into the first phase. Many die halfway through life." Now you have got to understand something. Sometimes people look at Psalms 90, and they think we are promised seventy to eighty years. But Psalms 90 was written by Moses, so that everybody that was twenty years and older was dead and gone so they could get into the promise land. That is what Psalms 90 is about. But Genesis 6:3 talks to us about 120 years. So mid-way is between 55 maybe 65. Pay very close attention. That is when a lot of ministers who are not getting to some things start getting into trouble. Pay attention because you can get on the other side of that.

So he said, "Many of my ministers will live and die and never get into the first phase." So, if he said it is important for you to get into every phase and every room, then it must be important for all of us to get into all of our phases and all of our rooms.

72

So he invited Elisha into his room. I think many would agree that Elisha helped Elijah; he ministered to him; he followed him. I think many would also agree that Elijah walked by Elisha. He cast his mantle on him. That represented the anointing coming on him and Elisha was ready to serve in that capacity.

The Lord will give you glimpses of your future. The Lord is letting you know what is ahead of you so you will prepare. Unfortunately sometimes people get confused. They will sense an anointing to do certain things, but just because you sense an anointing it does not mean the person is ready to flow in that. It is just the call. So we want to develop into some certain things. A lot of the things that all of us have done, we have grown through them. I am not saying, do not do anything until you are fully grown; we would never do anything.

2 Kings 2:9

And it came to pass, when they were gone over, that Elijah said unto Elisha, Ask what I shall do for thee, before I be taken away from thee. And Elisha said, I pray thee, let a double portion of thy spirit be upon me.

In 2 Kings 2:9, Elisha asked for a double portion. Many would agree with me when I say that he got it.

2 Kings 5:1

Now Naaman, captain of the host of the king of Syria, was a great man with his master, and honourable, because by him the LORD had given deliverance unto Syria: he was also a mighty man in valour, but he was a leper.

2 Kings 5:1 takes place after Elijah has left planet Earth so Elisha is walking in a certain office. He asked for a double portion and has grown through some things, different things. But now notice here in 2 Kings 5:1, the bible says, "Now Nahum, captain of the host of king of Syria, was a great man with his Master, honorable, because by him the Lord had given deliverance unto Syria. He was also a mighty man of valor, but he was a leper." We also know that they had captured a little handmaiden, and she must have known about the Prophet because she said, "I wish my Master was in the land over here because there is a man of God." So, undoubtedly, Elisha must have had a reputation of having a healing ministry?

Borrowed Anointing

2 Kings 5:9-10

9So Naaman came with his horses and with his chariot, and stood at the door of the house of Elisha.

10And Elisha sent a messenger unto him, saying, Go and wash in Jordan seven times, and thy flesh shall come again to thee, and thou shalt be clean.

Now verse 9 says, "So Naaman came with his horses, his chariots, and he stood at the door of the house of Elisha. And Elisha sent a messenger." Elisha sent Gehazi. Many would agree with me that undoubtedly, Gehazi was supposed to be just like Elisha. Elisha wanted Gehazi to do exactly what he had done to Elijah. So, undoubtedly, there must have been times that Elijah would have Elisha do something similar to what Elisha was now doing with Gehazi. And he asked Gehazi, he said, "You go out and you tell this man to go wash." The word "messenger" is "M-A-L-A-K". The root meaning is

74

to dispatch as a deputy or an as ambassador. That is what the "messenger" word here means. Gehazi was being taught the flows of the Holy Ghost. I call it a borrowed anointing. A borrowed anointing means there will be times when those that are in training and learning the anointing on whom they are following closely will come on them. Gehazi is not walking in the place of Elisha yet. But Elisha is in the tent and tells Gehazi, "You go tell him to go wash in the river." He went out, there had to have been an anointing. He was not operating by the anointing on him, he is now operating by the anointing of the one that he serves; it is a borrowed anointing. And so, there will be times when those that are in the ministry of helps and helping you, when they will, if they are close to you and they are faithful, there will be times when the anointing on you will fall, flow over on them.

We are trying to duplicate ourselves. We see this in the scripture; Our endeavor is to teach others what God has taught us. And then we want them to go further. Brother Hagin would teach us and say, "I would like for my ceiling to be your floor." I thought, "Dear God, are you kidding me?" But that is what he wanted. So we understand those principles. Many of us as natural parents always want our kids to do better than we did. It is just built in us. We want that. Well, spiritual parents want their spiritual kids to do better! And so, Elisha had experienced this, I am sure, over the years and what was on Elijah would come over on him. But, he did not ever, he did not move into that office until the day that he spoke to Elijah about it.

So Gehazi said, "Go wash." Naaman went and washed. Well, all of a sudden he saw Naaman come back; he is whole. He is like, "Oh my gosh! Oh my gosh! Did you all see that? I told him to go wash. Did you see that?" And they will come back excited. "You know, we went to the nursing home, you told us to go; we laid hands on somebody; they got healed!" Then all of a sudden, they want to start a ministry. They are not in their anointing yet. It is borrowed.

Years ago, a pastor friend of mine and another gentleman drove me back to the airport. On the way there I felt prompted by the Spirit of God. The Lord will show you things, but you cannot always just tell a person specifically, "This is where you are headed, you need to stop it." So you tell them a story and you hope they will get it. You know, sometimes they will leave the story and they will be like, "Boy that was a good story, I hope people hear that!" It was not for them, it was for you! So I begin to tell this one man that followed my pastor friend very, very closely, about Gehazi. I told hem about how he did this, and then all of a sudden when the Man of God did not take anything from Naaman, he said it is not the right time to receive gifts because just awhile ago, Naaman was so mad. He had been outside kicking dust, breaking sticks, kicking the camel, kicking the dog so on and so forth. "What do you mean I got to go wash in the creek? You know, we have got prettier rivers than they have got here!" He is ticked off. But now he is healed; now he wants to give. Wrong time. You just give people an opportunity to give before they ever receive anything; let them purpose in their heart what they want to give. Do not let everybody get healed or blessed then start receiving an offering. But anyway, got to be careful about money. Do not preach an hour and a half on money, and an hour and a half on the other message. But that is just my deal.

So all of a sudden, Naaman, leaves and Gehazi does his thing. We have no record that he had ever usurped authority before. He just moved over into a borrowed anointing. Now all of a sudden he thinks he is flowing. He is not flowing; he is in training diapers. And he says,

"My man of God just missed it! He let him leave here without getting clothing and all the stuff that he brought." Gehazi went after him. He was not flowing in his own anointing yet. He is only been able to do certain things either through the only anointing on him which is the ministry of helps, or when at times that those he is following closely just comes over on him for periods of time. But it does not stay.

So I tell the young man this in the car on the way to the airport. I also tell him about the borrowed anointing, hoping he will get it. But it was not long after that, that all of a sudden he rises up against my pastor friend and tries to take and do certain things. He thinks now he is a minister. Being called to be a minister is one thing, but just because you are called does not mean you are ready yet. So if you are called to be a pastor, more than likely, God will put you underneath a true pastor to mentor you, to impart things unto you. You will begin to experience things from that office of the shepherd that you are submitted to, but you do not have an anointing on you yet, it is a borrowed anointing. The day will come. Joshua sat on the side of the mountain 40 days waiting for Moses, and when Moses came back down, Joshua still sat in his right place! But the day came when Joshua was no longer the ministry of helps; the day came when he got to live out the dream that God gave him!

That young man does not even go to church now. Many believed that someday he would have been a pastor. But, he moved too quick. I remember when we went to Rhema. After the very first year I got to bugging God. I said, "Where in the world do you want me to go? Where do you want me to go?" This was burning in me, "People are dying and going to hell, I need to hurry up and get out there." So I start bugging God about, "Where am I going? Where am I going?" And finally God says, "Stop bugging me about where you are going." He said, "Do not you think I knew this was a two year school when I sent you?" and he said, "You have only attended one year, why in the world do you want to know now what is ahead of you when you have not even completed what I told you to do yet?"

Chapter 5: Rivers Vs. the Well

John 7:37-38

37In the last day, that great day of the feast, Jesus stood and cried, saying, If any man thirst, let him come unto me, and drink.

38He that believeth on me, as the scripture hath said, out of his belly shall flow rivers of living water.

39(But this spake he of the Spirit, which they that believe on him should receive: for the Holy Ghost was not yet given; because that Jesus was not yet glorified.)

John 7:37 says, "In the last day, that great day of the feast, Jesus stood, cried saying, 'If any man thirst let him come unto me and drink." That is the well on the inside of you. We are to learn to drink from the well in us. But then he said, "He that believeth on me as the scripture said out of his belly shall flow rivers of living water." Verse 39 says, "But this spake he of the spirit which say that breathe on him should receive, for the Holy Ghost was not yet given, because that Jesus was not yet glorified." The well is for us personally. The wells are ours personally to drink from, and the rivers are for service to others. Do we drink out of the river? No, we drink from the well. I want to prove something to you because sometimes people get confused with some things.

2 Kings 13:20-22

20And Elisha died, and they buried him. And the bands of the Moabites invaded the land at the coming in of the year.

21And it came to pass, as they were burying a man, that, behold, they spied a band of men; and they cast the man into the sepulchre of Elisha: and when the man was let down, and touched the bones of Elisha, he revived, and stood up on his feet.

22But Hazael king of Syria oppressed Israel all the days of Jehoahaz.

2 Kings 13:20 says, "And Elisha died. And they buried him. And the bands of the Moabite invaded the land at the coming of the year, and it came to pass as they were burying a man that behold they spied a band of man, and they cast the man into the sepulcher of Elisha. And when the man was let down and touched the bones of Elisha," what happened? "he revived and stood up on his feet." My question to you is; "How come Elisha died?" The possibilities are old age, sickness. What raised the young man that died up from the dead was the river. There was still enough residue of the anointing upon in his bones to raise somebody from the dead, but yet he died.

But, there was enough anointing in his dry bones to raise a man still from the dead. The river is not for you and I to drink from. I have studied these people that God used mightily. I have studied their lives; I studied Katherine Coleman; I have studied Marie Woodworth Etter ; I have studied William Branham; I have studied Jack Coe. and most of them, if you will look, a lot of them died in there thirties and forties. Katherine lived the longest. I think she lived to her mid sixties But she struggled with sickness. They learned to flow with the river, but they

80

wanted to also drink from the river. And Brother Hagin told all of them, he said, "All of you are building your ministries on gifts of the spirit, I am building mine on the word, I will still be here when you are gone because you are building yours on the gifts, I am building mine on the word."

We are going to drink from the well. So that is why we followed Brother Hagin so closely. How many of you know he told us, he said, "If you hear I am gone, know that no sickness got me, know I got satisfied." Smith, the man Brother Hagin followed closely, Smith Wigglesworth, never met him personally but read after him, he took off when he was 87. Dad Hagin stayed until he was 88, just to show he could. I remember, they would teach us some things. I remember, the book he had us read, *John Alexander Dowie*. He said, "You can follow people's faith, but sometimes you cannot follow their doctrine. Because wherever they get off doctrinally, you will get off too. But you can follow people's faith." And he said, "If you are not careful, the exact same age they died, you will die."

Getting back to Elisha. He just started his ministry, just kicked it off. Elijah just left, and then he showed up and they talked about the water being bad and he healed the waters. That, from what we can tell, was the first miracle. Next thing you know he is walking along and some kids start making fun of him. Then, there was the women who, with her husband's approval, built Elisha a chamber. One day, as he lay on the bed, out of his office, he said he wanted to bless her. He did not have a leading of the Holy Ghost because he did not know what she did, have, or needed. He asked his servant to look into it. He said, "She is been very careful for us, go see." The servant asked her, "Do you want us to talk to the governor? "No." "How about you need any…"

81

"No" Finally the servant said, "She does not have a child." Well, out of his office he was able to say some things.

This is some more of what God taught me that night in the truck. He said, "You are going to have to be learning some things about your word because the stronger the power on you, the stronger and quicker the evidence you are going to have when you say some things."

2 Kings 2:23-24 *Interesting*

23And he went up from thence unto Bethel: and as he was going up by the way, there came forth little children out of the city, and mocked him, and said unto him, Go up, thou bald head; go up, thou bald head.

24And he turned back, and looked on them, and cursed them in the name of the LORD. And there came forth two she bears out of the wood, and tare forty and two children of them.

Elisha healed the waters and as soon as he took off they started making some fun of him. Out of his office, it came to pass about some children; that is why we have to learn some things about the power that we are actually beginning to flow in. Here is the part I want you to see. "He went up from thence unto Bethel and as he was going up by the way, there came forth little children out of the city and they mocked him and said unto him go up thou bald head." Now I want you to think about something. Brother Hagin taught us this; he taught us several things from the outward man as perishing. He said, "How come he is bald?" The river would not help him there. How come he died? He died because he still lived in a natural body. The river would not help him. How come he does not have hair? It must have bothered him; he asked two bears to come and get them that talked about him. You know if you got hair and you shave it off and somebody calls you

82

a baldy it does not bother you. There are others that do not have hair and they like it. So, many would undoubtedly agree, he must have not liked not having hair because he got two bears to eat about 40 something kids. So, how come he, being a prophet, walking in the power of God, how come, he did not have hair? You have to drink from the well. You have to drink from the well.

2 Corinthians 4:16

For which cause we faint not; but though our outward man perish, yet the inward man is renewed day by day.

In 2 Corinthians 4:16 we read, "Our outward man is perishing, but the inward man is being renewed." I am hoping it is not just me, but I have discovered the older you get, there are certain parts of your body that will turn. Well, I am not going to let my words trip me up, but we are getting older. You know, things begin to sag; things begin to droop, different things. It does. But on the inside we are getting stronger and stronger. The river is not going to help me there? That is why I am encouraging ministers to find out about the rooms and phases now before old age creeps in.

2 Kings 3:10-13

10And the king of Israel said, Alas! that the LORD hath called these three kings together, to deliver them into the hand of Moab!

11But Jehoshaphat said, Is there not here a prophet of the LORD, that we may enquire of the LORD by him? And one of the king of Israel's

servants answered and said, Here is Elisha the son of Shaphat, which poured water on the hands of Elijah.

12And Jehoshaphat said, The word of the LORD is with him. So the king of Israel and Jehoshaphat and the king of Edom went down to him.

13And Elisha said unto the king of Israel, What have I to do with thee? get thee to the prophets of thy father, and to the prophets of thy mother. And the king of Israel said unto him, Nay: for the LORD hath called these three kings together, to deliver them into the hand of Moab.

Now 2 Kings 3:10 says here, "And the kings of Israel, said 'alas' that the king had called his 3 kings together, to deliver them into the hand of the Moab. But Jehoshaphat said, 'is there not here a prophet of the Lord we may inquire of the Lord by him?' And one of the king of Israel servants answered and said, 'here is Elisha son of Shaphat, which poured water on the hands of Elijah." He used to serve Elijah, but now he is flowing in what Elijah did." And so we see here, and "Jehoshaphat said the word of the Lord's with him, so the king of Israel, the king of Jehoshaphat and the king of Edom, went down to him." Continuing with, verse 13, "And Elisha said unto the king of Israel, 'what have I to do with thee? Get thee to the prophet of thy father." Well, it must not have been a prophet of God. "Why are you wanting to inquire of God now? Why do not you go back to those you have been talking to, or those that you have chosen to hook up with?" We got in trouble; this is not working. That is why it is important to stay with who God hooked you up with? Before my wife and I got saved, we would always say this, "Dance with the ones that brought you." Well, stay hooked up with those that God hooked you up with. Sometimes people will get a crazy idea and they will start saying things along the line; they will say it out of ignorance, but they will say things like, "Well, you know God is doing a new thing." New in regard to what? Separate from the spirit of God? Separate from the word of God? If we leave the word, if we leave the spirit, we cannot go and do what God has asked us to do, because that is how God does it to the body, or through the body of Christ. So then, stay with the one that brought you.

2 Kings 3:13-17

13And Elisha said unto the king of Israel, What have I to do with thee? get thee to the prophets of thy father, and to the prophets of thy mother. And the king of Israel said unto him, Nay: for the LORD hath called these three kings together, to deliver them into the hand of Moab.

14And Elisha said, As the LORD of hosts liveth, before whom I stand, surely, were it not that I regard the presence of Jehoshaphat the king of Judah, I would not look toward thee, nor see thee.

15But now bring me a minstrel. And it came to pass, when the minstrel played, that the hand of the LORD came upon him.

16And he said, Thus saith the LORD, Make this valley full of ditches.

17For thus saith the LORD, Ye shall not see wind, neither shall ye see rain

Then he says, "go back to the prophet of your father and the prophet of thy mother.' And the king of Israel said unto him, 'Nay for the Lord hath called these 3 kings together to deliver them in the hand of Moab.' Elisha said, 'as the Lord of hosts liveth before whom I stand surely were it not that I regard the presence of Jehoshaphat, the King of Judah. I would not look toward thee."

Now I want you to please make a note of this and write something down that will help you remember. Because 2 of the kings were not familiar with the flow of the Holy Ghost, they were ignorant of how the Holy Ghost moves or flows, they thought they could come into the presence of God any way they wanted to and receive from the flow of the Holy Ghost. In the book, *Understanding the Anointing,* Brother Hagin explains in great depth about this story. He talks about two who came in a backslidden state into the presence of Elisha but because of their condition, he had great difficulty getting over into his office because of their presence or, because of how they came into his presence wanting a flow of the Holy Ghost.

People will come to church many different ways, and many times that is why you will hit something or you will have difficulty getting over into your office or into the flow. We encourage people if they just had a fistfight, come on in, just do not cause an outbreak, but go ahead and come. But, the whole congregation ought to not have been fighting before we get there. We encourage people, "You come like you are! And the word will fix you." The word will fix you, if you will yield to it, if you will do it. We have done it ourselves.

But, because they were so ignorant of how the spirit of God moves, they thought they could get the exact same result of increase that God wants you and I to have by the word, by coming or going another direction. And God said that the man of God could not get into his office because of their condition. So he said, "Call me a minstrel that can help me get over into my office." The minstrel played, and," what happened? "the hand of the Lord came on him."

86

I remember in Odessa, Texas we were there where Brother T.L. Osborn's Sister, Daisy, started a church, Highwood Temple Assembly of God. I recall ministering there, and the Lord said, "There are people here with some back trouble." So I gave that word. Some people came forward and we were standing there ministering. As soon as I touched this lady, the spirit of God said to me, "Under the present circumstances, she cannot receive anything." I said, "Why?" you know, to myself, not out loud. And he said, "She is holding unforgiveness." So I said to her, "Ma'am," and I took my hands off because there was no need to be praying anymore. You cannot ever go past the word of God and expect to get the results of God. So I said to her, "Ma'am, are you holding unforgivess?" and she screamed at me, "No, I am not holding unforgiveness and you pray for me!" I thought, "Yeah, I hit a nerve! You should not have screamed at me, everybody knows God is right." And so I said, "Well ma'am it seemed like the Lord spoke to me." And you know, we are not saying that we never miss it. I mean give people the opportunity to say, "Yeah, you did or you did not." But, it was evident that the Holy Ghost did and that I heard the Holy Ghost right. He never misses it, but he flows through us and sometimes we miss hearing.

So I said, "Well ma'am, I cannot go passed the word of the lord and so I cannot pray for you if there is unforgiveness. I could, but we are not going to get any results." So we were standing there and I started to move on. Brother Cecil was standing there beside me. She looked at him and this is what she said, "Brother Cecil, you make him pray for me right now!" She is so oblivious to how the Holy Ghost flows that she thinks she can come any way and still get what God says belongs to her. There are conditions on how God flows.

Back home in Oklahoma we have lighting storms, thunderstorms. You would not exercise good sense if a thundercloud comes up and as you see lighting strike you grab a metal pole and hold it up in the air and run outside. You are going to get a flow that you really do not want. If you try to pursue or push to still get a flow that is not according to the word, you will get a flow, but it will not be the flow that you are looking for. So finally I told her, "You are going to have to gimp your crippled self on back down and sit down". I mean really, so she gimped, hobbled back to her seat. She came crippled; she left cripple.

There is a flow to the Holy Ghost. You as pastors, will get up and preach a message; God will give you a message; you know it is hot off the wire and you know it is going to apply to some people in the church. You might not know exactly who it is, but you know by the unction or the flow that the Holy Ghost is nailing hides to the wall. Then all of a sudden, somebody gets their lip pouched out and they get mad, and they will be like, "Well who does he think he is? He is trying to tell me how to live!" They are so ignorant of how the Holy Ghost flows, they immediately associate to some person trying to quench them having fun, and they do not even recognize it as a flow of the Holy Ghost!

Acts 6:1

1And in those days, when the number of the disciples was multiplied, there arose a murmuring of the Grecians against the Hebrews, because their widows were neglected in the daily ministration.

2Then the twelve called the multitude of the disciples unto them, and said, It is not reason that we should leave the word of God, and serve tables.

3Wherefore, brethren, look ye out among you seven men of honest report, full of the Holy Ghost and wisdom, whom we may appoint over this business.

Acts 6:1 says, "And in those days when the number of disciples was multiplied, there arose a murmuring of the Grecian among the Hebrews because their widows are being neglected, in the daily administration. Then the twelve called a multitude of disciples unto them and said is it not reason that we should leave the word of God and serve tables? Wherefore look you out seven men full are honest report and full of the Holy Ghost." We have to ask ourselves if the leadership understood the flow of the Holy Ghost. Yes. But sometimes people do not. The leadership did here but sometimes not. But this is for teaching purposes of what we have been talking about. Sometimes people will think, "Well cannot you mow the grass, drive the van, oversee the food ministry, and do this, and do that, and still preach?" No, you cannot. "They will say, "Cannot you still preach? Cannot you oversee the food ministry? Cannot you run all this food all over town, because you know this is your job?" No it is not. The office of the shepherd is to feed the flock. That is the job. That is the job description, not be the hired hand. Thank God the leadership knew the flow of the Holy Ghost.

And so they immediately said, "No! We should not leave the word which brought the increase, and start serving the increase. So, look you out seven men of honest report, full of the Holy Ghost that we may appoint over this business." I can say that many of us are grateful for the Ministry of Helps.

I have talked about it before and I will say it again. The day before the president was elected, there was nothing wrong with him mowing his own lawn, filling up his gas tank, or going to the grocery store. But the Day after he was elected president, it is not that he is above doing these things, but his office now is higher? He is called the president of the United States. There are more important things that are assigned to his office than running the food ministry. There are more important things assigned to his office than mowing the yard. He is not our gardener; he is the president of the United States! There are thing that have to do with our country he needs to be looking at! Your pastor has to have time to get into the word of God and hear from heaven and trust the Holy Ghost. And when he comes to the pulpit he is got something fresh right off, hot from the wire of the Holy Ghost! And it is something that will change you, help you, fix you and give you answers. That is the flow of the Holy Ghost. And when ministers understand this, if that is the flow of the Holy Ghost then we immediately understand, "Okay there is a flow of the Holy Ghost of Elijah and Elisha. A Paul and a Timothy, a Moses and a Joshua." Amen!

I know at Six Flags and other places, they have a house called, "The House of Gravity." It is an optical illusion because they will put a ball in what looks like a gutter or something and it looks like that ball will take off and go uphill and roll out over somewhere else. But, nonetheless, gravity is still working. If you go outside and climb up in a tree, and you jump out, you are not just going to float around like a bird, you are going to smack the ground. Gravity is still working. Well, then, there must be a flow of the Holy Ghost. There are certain things that will enhance the flow, and there are certain things that will stop the flow. Electricians, they know, I have had them work on some stuff that we have. Most electricians have told me, "We like to work with wire while it is still hot, because if we ever think its dead we become careless. So we treat it as if it is hot all the time." They understand the flow of electricity. "There are laws it will not violate. It will flow certain ways so if that line up there needs to be patched and tied to this one," they say, "Immediately we understand there is a flow of the Holy Ghost. So I can stand on the ground with a fiberglass pole and rubber gloves and I can handle something that is hot and it will never ever affect me because there are certain laws to certain flows." But they said, "Never can we stand on the ground and use a metal pole because that is a conductor and it will flow through that. We cannot handle it no more, now it is flowing to us." There are certain things God wants to flow to the body through us. Through us! It is not us; it is through us.

So there are certain things we have got to learn to do so that we do not stop the flow, but instead allow the FLOW of the POWER of the conduit to come through us and get to the family of God. It is not our power, but it is just flowing through us. And when people come forward and the Lord says, "You know they are mad at Sister Bertha or somebody like that," the Holy Ghost is not trying to embarrass them; he is trying to get a flow of the Holy Ghost to him. But there is a wall there; there is a rubber pole there and he cannot get to them because that has to be dealt with. He loves them so much, He wants a flow so He tells you, "Get that out of their life or let them deal with it!" Thank God for the flow of the Holy Ghost.

Chapter 6: Spiritual Equipment

The Five fold Ministry offices will always have certain gifts or equipment that will go with that office. in an old manual, *The Ministry Gifts*, by Kenneth E. Hagin, you will find an abundance of resources that God gave him and that we can use. In the beginning of this manual, it talks about ministry gifts with ministry offices. It says, "Layman can have spiritual gifts operating through them, but ministers will be equipped to minister regular with those gifts necessary to stand in their office because they are called to it. The same spiritual gifts operating through the ministerial level will always carry a greater anointing."

I Corinthians 12:28

28And God hath set some in the church, first apostles, secondarily prophets, thirdly teachers, after that miracles, then gifts of healings, helps, governments, diversities of tongues.

Ephesians 4:8, 11-12

8Wherefore he saith, When he ascended up on high, he led captivity captive, and gave gifts unto men.

11And he gave some, apostles; and some, prophets; and some,

evangelists; and some, pastors and teachers;

12For the perfecting of the saints, for the work of the ministry, for the edifying of the body of Christ:

1 Corinthians 12:28 says, "And God has set some in the church, first apostles, secondarily prophets, thirdly teachers, after that miracles, gifts of healings, helps, governments, and diversity of tongues." Ephesians 4 says, "Jesus lead captivity captive, gave gifts unto men." First there is apostles, prophet, evangelists, pastors and teachers. "And he gave them to the body for the perfecting of the saints so that the saints might do the work of the ministry." So where is the Layman in all of this? Well we find them in the ministry of helps. Here is what the Lord helped me understand. Brother Hagin explains that in November 28, 1938 Jesus visited him. At that time Jesus told him, "I have given unto you a gift of healing. I have sent you to minister to the sick." Brother Hagin admits he had not done much about that and found that 10 years had gone by. As a pastor he would have supernatural occurrences once in awhile. He knew the spirit of God was moving in this way and they would have some supernatural manifestations and healings. He would recall that the last church he had pastored he had shut himself up in the church to seek God. Here the Lord told him, "The reason that you are not satisfied in your spirit is because I never called you to pastor to begin with." Here the Lord said to him, "What are you going to do about what I said to you in that home 10 years ago? When I said to you that I have given you the gift of healing.

Getting back to what the bible says about gifts. The bible says, "gifts of healing," in plural form. Jesus did not tell Brother Hagin, "gifts of healing." He said, "a gift". In order to be clear I need to explain a few things about Brother Hagin. When he and Sister Oretha got married,

93

his father-in-law and mother-in-law asked them to move in with them in order to save some money. He joked that he had a dime after they got married so he bought two nickel candy bars, one for her, one for him, and they ate them and went broke and started out. He said it was a wonderful Methodist home. One evening, as they were getting ready to go to bed, they all gathered to pray. The spirit of the Lord began to deal with him and told him, "I have given you a gift."

I Corinthians 12:7-9

7But the manifestation of the Spirit is given to every man to profit withal.

8For to one is given by the Spirit the word of wisdom; to another the word of knowledge by the same Spirit;

9To another faith by the same Spirit; to another the gifts of healing by the same Spirit;

When you start looking at the gifts in 1 Corinthians 12, it says, "for to one is given one," one gift at a time. But with a ministry office, there are several gifts given to accompany that office. But through laity, a gift is never given only the manifestation. That is what verse 7 says. But the manifestation of the spirit is given. But see with the office of a Pastor, there ought to be several gifts to accompany, to help with that office.

Brother Hagin told us, "If I was a Pastor, I would pray for diversity of tongues and interpretation of tongues." Because scripture says, "If there be a group of people somebody give a message in tongue, but there be not interpreter, let him who is going to give the message keep silent," So if that gift is given to a pastor, then many people can be assuredly if they have a message in tongues, the pastor can always interpret. And, if he is given the opportunity to interpret it will come on a higher revelation. Then there ought to be at times gifts of healing flowing through the pastor. We are not saying that there are not nor that they all cannot, but there ought to be some gifts that accompany certain offices to qualify that office. But to the laity, no gift is ever given, only the manifestation. OK, I See!

I Corinthians 1:2

Unto the church of God which is at Corinth, to them that are sanctified in Christ Jesus, called to be saints, with all that in every place call upon the name of Jesus Christ our Lord, both their's and our's:

I Corinthians 12:31

But covet earnestly the best gifts: and yet shew I unto you a more excellent way. Love

1 Corinthians 1:2 says. "Unto the church of God, which is at Corinth." The letter is written to the whole church. So when you look at 12:31, it says to covet, crave, desire the best gifts. Whichever one is best needed at the time. So the responsibility in a local assembly to covet, crave and desire the manifestation of the gifts falls on the whole church as the letter is written to the whole church. So if the whole church family covets, craves, and desires the gifts, then the Holy Ghost feels welcomed enough to show up. When people say, "We do not have the gifts anymore." They need to ask themselves if they covet them, if they want them. Or is it an embarrassment because it will drive people away? I do not mean to be hard, but these things have to be said! We are ministers; we can hear these things.

So he says in verse 31 to covet earnestly. We know the church is our Lord Jesus Christ's church and that he died for this church. He was the body when he was here, but when he died, Galatians says he was no longer the body; he became the head. Everybody that gets saved makes up the body! So I should not change the direction of the body if it does not come from the head. Many leaders may get to thinking the church is theirs. It is not theirs; it is Jesus' and if he says these things profit my church these things help my family, if they will bring a profit, if they will help and the head of the church said so, I should not let my little infinite pea-brain ever think it is smarter than the head of the church.

I Corinthians 12:1

Now concerning spiritual gifts, brethren, I would not have you ignorant.

Verse 1 says, "Now concerning things of the spirit brethren, do not be ignorant." We all know what ignorant is, unlearned, no knowledge, unknowing. If knowledge shows up and you still do not do it, now you are stupid. To be unknowing, that is one thing. To be taught certain things where God hooks you up and you become so educated and then it is not important… that makes you stupid! I would rather have the Baptist; I would rather have the Baptist and the Methodist come to my meetings. They will not fight me near as hard because they are just ignorant. If you can show them in the word most of them will go with you but those that have been there and have become so educated they will fight you on it because they are not ignorant, they are stupid!

I Corinthians 12:2

Ye know that ye were Gentiles, carried away unto these dumb idols,

even as ye were led.

So then he says, right after do not be ignorant about spiritual things, he immediately says, "Listen, every leading is not of God! Do not be lead unto dumb idols or things that you think have life or have the ability to take you somewhere, stay with the Holy Ghost, and stay with what the head of the church said would profit the church!" I am still a young man; I know where I am headed; I do not think I am there yet, though. And I am not trying to be negative, but it takes time to get to places. It takes time to grow into certain things. Just understand this: Whatever bothers God will always bother the prophet. Whatever is going on in a church family will always bother the shepherd. If there is something going on in the family, it ought to bother the parents; they will pick it up; they will perceive it. Whatever bothers God will bother the prophet. And many times, what is bothering God will come through that office. He will want to correct some things through teaching. So I am not mad or trying to be negative. I just do not like people that are stupid. They are harder to deal with than people that are ignorant.

If given the opportunity, you can take somebody who does not know the word of God lead them to salvation. There is this story about a young Christian who sat next to a Buddhist on a plane ride for several hours. Her friend took her bible out, started in the book of Genesis, went through it, and taught the Buddhist passenger about what it was to believe in Jesus. Her friend had this guy saved! He was not stupid; he was ignorant! When light starts coming, if you are smart, you will go with the light!

I Corinthians 12:7-9

7But the manifestation of the Spirit is given to every man to profit

withal.

8For to one is given by the Spirit the word of wisdom; to another the word of knowledge by the same Spirit;

9To another faith by the same Spirit; to another the gifts of healing by the same Spirit;

Verse 7 says, "But the manifestation of the spirit is given to every man to profit withal." There are some translations that say, "Help the entire church." If it is going to profit withal, it is going to help the whole church. Still other translations say, "For the common good." The gifts are the manifestations of the gift for the common good. If they are sent to help, I want them.

Verse 8 says, "For to one is given." The church family as a whole can covet and crave and desire, "Lord we want the manifestation of the gifts of the spirit in our midst." Because this is a sovereignty of God, we cannot tell what gift, nor whom He will use in what gift; our job is to covet, crave and desire for Him to show up.

If there is a message in tongues which needs interpretation, we ought to be thankful and expect to hear from heaven; we ought to be excited that our Pastor is going to have a word from heaven to teach us; we must expect that he is going to feed us; he is our shepherd. Then we need to say, "Lord we covet and crave the gifts of the spirit." If someone comes in sick, He might have a word of knowledge, "Somebody is here with a bad back." With that, since he is a pastor, it will be more than just one gift at a time, there could be a word of knowledge with a gift of healing, and that person can leave out of that service healed. That just helped the church.

I remember one time I was preaching and the Lord said, "Somebody is here that had a broken back and different things." A lady got up, and when she came to the front was so drunk I could smell it on her breath. She came to the front staggering. I did not know it immediately and thought she was under the power of God, but when she stood before me since I used to drink, immediately I knew what she was under. She was under the influence of alcohol. I remember thinking in my head immediately, "She is not going to get anything, she is drunk!" But God called it out. When I went to touch her she fell. I did not know whether she passed out or the power hit her. I was not sure. When she got up, they helped her back up and she staggered back to her seat. I got back to preaching and all of a sudden she raised her hand, "Can I say something?" and I said "Oh no, now what?" And she said, "Can I now get saved?" That helped the church. That manifestation of the gift helped the church. And then she taught Sunday school for us for I do not know how many years. I mean, you talk about a good one; she was a good one. She had come in ignorant, but she was open.

Bonus Chapter - Room of the Unlearned

Becoming Skillful

Acts 4:13

[13]Now when they saw the boldness of Peter and John, and perceived that they were unlearned and ignorant men, they marvelled; and they took knowledge of them, that they had been with Jesus.

The word "unlearned" in Acts 4:13, means more than not able to write your name. There was a school by the Jewish nation called the school of the Papyri and it was a place that provided instruction on theology and Jewish doctrine. So when these men said "unlearned", what they meant was these guys never went to the Jewish School, but yet, they perceive they had been with Jesus.

We are never opposed to education. One of the things with our children, years gone by, there were some people that tried to make me and my wife feel bad because we never felt very strong about sending any of our children to college. I said, "Why would I ever raise up a child in the house of God, and then pay somebody to discredit what took us 18 years to put in them?" "Well they need a degree!" No, they need to do whatever God's asked them to do. I'm not against education; there are some careers that people need an educated for or need a degree to be able to flow there. So we're not opposed to education. I've known some people that had to go to school to get a certain degree and they have told me personally that some of the things they were taught were not right, but they had to be there to get the degree to be able to do what they felt God asked them to do. They were settled enough in the word of God that they would not let what they learned shake them in what they believe.

Christianity is based upon faith. If you explained to somebody the life of Jesus, it would take faith to believe that he was born from a woman who had never been with a man. It would take faith to know that Jesus walked the Earth for 30 years then healed many people and did great things to be crucified and descend into hell. Not only that, but he rose on the third day and picked up his body to show to many people for forty days and left on a cloud while angels proclaimed he would come back the same way. You can't prove that to anybody. What we see in the word of God, is a faith based belief. There are people that have tried to prove that the Word of God is just another book. To those that do not have the spirit of God, or refuse to believe in it, it's just another autobiography or history book. To those who do believe, it's God speaking to them. It's a faith based belief.

In Acts 4:13, what they perceived was that they were not educated in Jewish doctrine, but yet they understood the things of the spirit.

In 1 Corinthians 14, it talks about the room of the unlearned. Quite often, many are in a room of the unlearned. It doesn't mean that they do not know how to write their name, it means they don't understand the flow of the spirit. In Acts 4:13, the New Living Translation says

"They could see that they were ordinary men, with no special training in the scriptures or from education or school."

1 Corinthians 14:12

[12]Even so ye, forasmuch as ye are zealous of spiritual gifts, seek that ye may excel to the edifying of the church.

In 1 Corinthians 14:12, the word "Excel," means to accelerate, or grow the fastest way possible, Another translation reads, "Since you are so eager to have special abilities that the spirit gives, seek those that will strengthen the whole church."

Zeal is wonderful, but education needs to go along with it. It's not an education natural things, but an understanding of things of the spirit. Zeal without knowledge will not edify the church and many times, it will create confusion.

I've known people who became very zealous to do something for God. A young man, years gone by, came to us off of drugs and other vices and stayed with us for awhile. He came to me and he said, "I'm going to go minister; I'm going to go tell the youth what not to do." And I said, "No. Brother you don't qualify yet." He said, "Yeah, but I'm just so hot with God!"

I said, "Brother, you're full of zeal, but you're unlearned. If you go talk to all the youth right now, and then you don't stay stable, they're going to wonder why I had you get up. You stay faithful for 6 months and then come see me again."

"Well I feel like I'm supposed to go!"

I said, "That's the Holy Ghost, he's telling you! But he's telling you so you'll prepare yourself."

He was zealous, but he didn't understand the things of the spirit. Many feel the tug to minister to people, but they refuse to stay under somebody to learn about the spirit.

The devil tried to kill me there. I had a burning desire to preach, but the Lord instructed me to go to school first. I wondered, "What about all the people that are going to hell?" and I preached a few times, and thank God none of them were recorded. They were rough, and they were not very deep. Again, the Lord said, "If you would go to school, I can teach you more in two years than what you would learn in ten or twelve on your own. You may not even finish because you'll get discouraged, but if I can build a foundation in you then you'll be able to stay."

The zeal is to help the body of Christ, and there should be understanding of the things of the spirit to add to it.

1 Corinthians 14:23-24

23If therefore the whole church be come together into one place, and all speak with tongues, and there come in those that are unlearned, or unbelievers, will they not say that ye are mad?

24But if all prophesy, and there come in one that believeth not, or one unlearned, he is convinced of all, he is judged of all:

In 1 Corinthians 14:23, There a distinct difference between someone who is unlearned and someone who does not believe. In the church, there are people who are unlearned about the things of the spirit, but it does not mean they're unbelievers. An unbeliever is somebody that has not been saved and has no working knowledge of the things of the spirit.

Verse twenty four reads, "But if all prophesy, and there come in one that believeth not or the unlearned, he's convinced of all, he is judged of all."

There are two distinct groups, the unlearned and the unbeliever. The word "unlearned" in 1 Corinthians 14 does not mean the same as "unlearned" in Acts 14. According to the Vine's Expository Dictionary, the word "unlearned" from 1 Corinthians means "ignoramus." It doesn't mean they're lost, it means they're ignorant. That refers to someone who is saved and attends church. Vine's also defines "unlearned" as "Somebody that's uninstructed, or a person without professional knowledge so they are unskilled." They have zeal, but they are not skillful.

Luke 13 tells about the woman who had a bad back. Everybody was trying to fix her bad back, but only Jesus perceived it as something of the spirit. Everybody else wanted to help her, but they did not know how. They were not skilled, they were unlearned, so they were trying to naturally fix a bad back. Jesus explained that to her that it was in the realm of the spirit, dealt with it, and the women who had been bent over for 15 years was able to stand up straight and walk around freely.

It is important to become very skillful in the things of the Spirit. Unskillful is defined as "Those with no knowledge in the area of unlearned, those with no knowledge of the facts relating to the testimony of the workings of God that you will find in and through the local church."

1 Colossians 1:9

⁹For this cause we also, since the day we heard it, do not cease to pray for you, and to desire that ye might be filled with the knowledge of his will in all wisdom and spiritual understanding;

He qualified when he gained the wisdom, because spiritual wisdom brings about spiritual understanding. If you were getting ready to work on a vacuum sweeper, you can read a manual and you're going to get knowledge, but it is not spiritual.

Song of Solomon 3:8

⁸They all hold swords, being expert in war: every man hath his sword upon his thigh because of fear in the night.

One of the definitions of "unlearned" was "unskilled." Song of Solomon 3:8, says that they all held swords and were expert and skilled.

Isaiah 3:3

³The captain of fifty, and the honourable man, and the counsellor, and the cunning artificer, and the eloquent orator.

Isaiah 3:3 talks about being skillful in speech. Zeal does not qualify anyone to be ready to go, but we should thank God for good zeal.

Jeremiah 46:9

⁹Come up, ye horses; and rage, ye chariots; and let the mighty men come forth; the Ethiopians and the Libyans, that handle the shield; and the Lydians, that handle and bend the bow.

The words "handle the shield" in the New Living Translation, are written as "skilled with the shield and the bow." If you believe with all of your heart that God has asked you to do something concerning His kingdom, you need zeal to do that. Without zeal, there will never really be a push to stay faithful and you will remain casual. People that have worked with me before have said, "Well that's good enough for people in Pawnee." When we take pride in what we're doing, we're not exalting ourselves, it means that we are honorable in what our end results look like. We give effort, we're not sloppy and we're skilled.

Romans 11:29

29For the gifts and calling of God are without repentance.

God says everybody in the body has a gift or a calling. The word "ungifted" doesn't mean they can't do anything, it means they never took time to become skilled.

When you are hired for a job, one of the first things the company will do is put you through training. You can go in there with zeal, excited you got a new job and wanting to provide for your family, but you need training.

I worked for Houston Pipeline Company after the rigs went down. They told me to dig out pipelines that were hot. They said they had to have the boxes. Down in Southeast Texas and Louisiana, the ground was so wet that they had built all these boxes, and there were also valves to cut off the flow if something blew up. We dug around 24 and 36 inch pipes that lead to Houston as well as other places. They asked me if I ever used a backhoe. I said I could, and then they asked if I could feel a tree root, and I said I could.

I sat on a Case backhoe for many hours and you can feel in the knobs when you hook a root. They told me that I had a job with them for as long as I wanted. We would dig up the pipes, and they would melt tar and pour it over the valves to prevent them from rusting. They explained to me that it was cheaper to do maintenance than to start all over. So I learned some things about becoming skilled in my profession.

If you're called to a local church and you support that church by helping in the ministry of helps, bringing your tithe and helping in the things of the spirit, then no matter what you feel like God's asked you to do, it will be blessed. It's not because you're a wonderful backhoe operator, but if you're skillful in the things of the spirit, everything else you touch is blessed. The confusing part for people is recognizing that they have an education, but it's not something of the spirit.

The room of the unlearned is a room for training to become a skilled, master craftsman in whatever God asked you to do.

By Invitation Only

1 Kings 19:16

[16]And Jehu the son of Nimshi shalt thou anoint to be king over Israel: and Elisha the son of Shaphat of Abelmeholah shalt thou anoint to be prophet in thy room.

The room of the unlearned is also the room of the ignorant. The word "unlearned", in this passage doesn't mean stupid, nor is it referring to someone who is not saved. However, there are those that do come into the room that are unbelievers.

People who do not believe in the movement of God's spirit are in the same category as the unbeliever. Things of the spirit cannot be taught to unbelievers because they are not in the spirit. It is amazing that some Christians are so ignorant of the spirit that they think it's the devil.

One night we were in Mexico, we ministered to several other ministers. Dad had me minister to four deaf people and they were healed; several people that were crippled were healed and one lady that Dad ministered to came out of her wheelchair. Many things transpired, and we were all ripped with the power of God. We went to eat at Chili's and the power of God fell. One minister got up and started dancing in the Holy Ghost. Another minister started praying to another minister, and he fell out in the aisle and was shaking on the floor. The rest of us were in a fog and the waiters and waitresses were looking at us and telling one another, "You go wait on them, I'm not going!" We were not trying to be a spectacle; it happened in the spirit. There was a young man from Chihuahua who came along to help us, and on the way back to our hotel he said the Lord told him to go back into Chili's. He went back to gather all of the waiters, waitresses and cooks together and explained what they saw. He spoke with them until three o'clock in the morning, and all of them were saved before he left.

When in a public setting, we should not be a spectacle and cause others to think we are not serious about God. Wherever I am, unless I am being held at gun point, I would cut loose for him. If I am being held by a gun and God tells me to dance, I'm going to dance and an angel will smack the man or take his gun away.

Elisha thought he was a farmer. Your spiritual leaders see things in you that God only reveals to them because of their leadership. Many times they will ask something of you, but what they are doing is inviting you into their room so you are no longer sitting in the room of the ignorant. They have been in this room themselves, they have worked with all the equipment and they understand it.

If you started a brand new job tomorrow, and you never worked with their type of technology, somebody who knows how to use all of the equipment will train you to use it. Their goal is not to make anyone feel stupid; they are trying to teach you to use the equipment that God has given you. Many times, people don't want to listen to instruction, and that's why Paul said "Let those that are unlearned still be unlearned. Let the things of the spirit be done without confusion."

When you first give a little boy a fake gun, you teach him how to use it. You give instructions and rules for that equipment because it can be dangerous to put equipment into zealous hands, anybody could get hurt.

When the Spirit of God is moving in a church service, Paul said, "God is not the author of confusion." He also said ,"But let the ignorant be ignorant still because they refuse to be taught when they're invited into a room to be taught how to work with this equipment or things of the spirit."

The prophet who invited Elisha into his room did not know Elisha. Rather, God had to tell him who he was and where to find him. The Man of God followed the instruction of God almighty. Elisha couldn't hear that he was called to help Elijah because he thought he was a farmer. The Man of God heard Heaven, and when he walked by and invited Elisha to follow him, he kept walking. We don't have time to wait 3 years for somebody to obey God and be faithful. The Man of

God had a mission; God told him what to do. He invited Elisha into his room to learn how to handle the equipment he was given.

He kept walking, and Elisha ran up and he said "Wait just a little bit, I need to run home." Elijah responded, "What have I done to you? I didn't call you; I just told you what God said. If you want to come, come on. If you don't, stay with your donkeys and asses and oxen and plow." He was not trying to be mean and crude, but he didn't call Elisha. God told him exactly what to do, and he only did that.

God will tell ministers to invite different people into their room. They will invite someone to go to a meeting, and sometimes they will respond with, "I don't have time." Many times the Lord will tell them not ask again. God sees something in them that needs to be developed through observation. They may not be invited to preach the message, but if God says "Come into the room," he will provide them with a gun. It may look real, but it's a play gun that they will be taught how to load, aim and shoot it.

2 Kings 2:12

¹²And Elisha saw it, and he cried, My father, my father, the chariot of Israel, and the horsemen thereof. And he saw him no more: and he took hold of his own clothes, and rent them in two pieces.

There were three times that Elijah said, "Why don't you wait right here?" Elisha said, "No, you invited me in, I've been with you all this time, I'm staying with you." Every other thing Elijah said to him was a command. If he'd have told him, "You wait here," being the servant he was, he would have waited, but Elijah asked him to wait.

110

Many times the Lord has told me to minister to someone specifically in a service. I'll ask them, "Are you going to be at church Wednesday night?" and they'd say "You know I don't know if I am or not." The Lord will say, "You can't tell them." People think we're concerned with numerical attendance, but it's about depth of the spirit. If Abraham stopped what was going to happen at Sodom and Gomorrah by himself, then we can change the United States with five people. The more allies you have, the stronger you can be. As for the things of the spirit, if it be God's will, he will use one man in a mighty way.

2 Kings 2:9

⁹And it came to pass, when they were gone over, that Elijah said unto Elisha, Ask what I shall do for thee, before I be taken away from thee. And Elisha said, I pray thee, let a double portion of thy spirit be upon me.

Elijah asked Elisha to wait, but he said, "No. If you tell me to I will but I know my assignment. I was invited into the room." Elijah asked, "Well what do you want then?" and Elisha responded, "Let a double portion of what you have be given to me".

He saw him, and then picked up the mantle of Elijah. He's not talking about physical dress. When the Man of God walked by and threw his mantle on him, that represented the anointing, and office in which he stood as a prophet. Elijah gave the mantle of a prophet to Elisha, but Elisha thought he was a farmer. It is believed that he served the Man of God for 15 years, possibly longer. It took him 15 years to learn how to use his equipment.

Isaiah 61:3

111

³To appoint unto them that mourn in Zion, to give unto them beauty for ashes, the oil of joy for mourning, the garment of praise for the spirit of heaviness; that they might be called trees of righteousness, the planting of the LORD, that he might be glorified.

There is a garment of praise that we are to put on when the devil's trying to take our peace. Some of us leave the garment of oppression on. The Man of God came by and put a different garment on Elisha, letting him know what the future beheld if he would be faithful.

People get tired of pushing against the things of the spirit and start to think being a saved Christian is enough. Any dead fish can float down stream, but it takes a live one to fight the current. The devil is on the bank with a variety of lures, trying to get you to bite on something and pull you out of the water. There are quite a few waterfalls and there are even some bears, but if you'll keep swimming, you can get through it.

Jeremiah 43:12

¹²And I will kindle a fire in the houses of the gods of Egypt; and he shall burn them, and carry them away captives: and he shall array himself with the land of Egypt, as a shepherd putteth on his garment; and he shall go forth from thence in peace.

In 1988, we started a church in Silsbee, Texas and I was asking the Lord for help. We worked on drilling rigs, and then we drove busses. We did several things, because faith will do whatever it takes to put food on the table and stay in a home.

The Lord began to lead me into some things in landscaping, and I loved to mow, but I told him I was not a landscaper. He said, "You're not trying to leave the calling of a minister, but you're doing something to enhance it so you can stay here and continue to develop your ministry. If you'll ask me, I'll give you a garment of landscaping."

People began to call saying they heard I was one of the best landscapers. I have never been to school for landscaping. One person asked if I could cut a wisteria into a bush. I wanted to say, "No," but I kept hearing 1 John 2:20, "You have an unction from the Holy One, you know all things." And I said, "You know what, yeah I sure can." I started cutting on one and began praying in tongues asking God to help me so I would not lose the job. I finished, and they came out and said it was the best job they have ever seen.

Mark 10:46-50

46And they came to Jericho: and as he went out of Jericho with his disciples and a great number of people, blind Bartimaeus, the son of Timaeus, sat by the highway side begging.

47And when he heard that it was Jesus of Nazareth, he began to cry out, and say, Jesus, thou son of David, have mercy on me.

48And many charged him that he should hold his peace: but he cried the more a great deal, Thou son of David, have mercy on me.

49And Jesus stood still, and commanded him to be called. And they call the blind man, saying unto him, Be of good comfort, rise; he calleth thee.

50And he, casting away his garment, rose, and came to Jesus.

Blind Bartimaeus heard the crowd yelling and asked what was going on. When he heard the Son of David was coming, he started hollering. He was told to keep quiet and he screamed louder. Jesus asked of his disciples to bring Blind Bartimaeus to him, and as he stood up, he threw off his garment.

There are many garments people wear in the church, but not all wear what God called them to wear. Many will stay in poverty, which is a garment. They will stay in oppression, because they don't understand praise. Blind Bartimaeus, who didn't know much, had enough sense to know if Jesus said, "Come I'm calling you." that he could get rid of whatever was on him, and something new was coming. He took the beggars garment off.

In church history, you couldn't panhandle like you do on the streets now. People will walk around holding a sign that says, "Vet," while standing on the corner. In earlier days, you had to go before an official and qualify to be able to panhandle. To qualify, they had to be blind, crippled or disabled and they would be given a different garment to wear. If they had the ability to work but refused to, they couldn't qualify. So when Blind Bartimaeus stood up, he took the garment off, threw it aside and was lead to Jesus. He may have been lead over, but he walked back by himself.

I never minded being lead by men and women that God put me under, I always submitted. I never felt little or unimportant, because they were putting things into me and teaching me how these things worked. I was very willing to be lead around by those that God put into my life. I never said, "Well I know that!" I'm becoming more and more skillful. They would always show me how to use new pieces of equipment.

We were at the lumber yard, before the old building blew away, and I was asked to help cut a piece. I said "Sure, yeah I can do that." I was down there for awhile 'with the table saw. I looked all over for a button, a switch or something but I couldn't get it to work.
It's a piece of equipment that I thought I knew how to operate. Finally I went to ask for help, I said, "How do you turn that thing on?" and He

said, "Oh I forgot to tell you, we put a kill button over on the wall over there."

You can spend quite a few years wandering around looking for the button, or you can become a master craftsman by learning from someone who is a master craftsman. You can hook up with somebody who knows more than you do in the things of the spirit. Your spiritual father, your pastor, can teach you some things about the Holy Ghost. As you listen, pay attention. It will take you way beyond your years.

Sunday nights when we don't have church, we tell people go be with their family. If there is another church they want to visit, we hope they enjoy themselves. Many have come back and said to me, "We went here to visit, and it was not the same." We are learning to be skillful with the things of the spirit.

2 Kings 2:13

[13]He took up also the mantle of Elijah that fell from him, and went back, and stood by the bank of Jordan;

Elisha took up the mantle of Elijah and ripped his own mantle apart. He told the prophet, "I want what's on you, I served you faithfully, I've watched you use the different pieces of equipment that come with your office. You told me in the beginning you saw in me the same office. I've served you for 15 years, I've had several invitations to go to other ministers and help them, but I've stayed true to you."

Those that serve in the ministry of helps need to know that the reason you look good and other ministres and ministries want you is because you are well trained. Their people are goofy because they're goofy

115

concerning the things of the spirit. You're good help because you understand things of the spirit.

Some will invite you to go and help them. Now if God says "Go," then you need to go. You've been faithful and you've helped. If you are trained in things of the spirit but if God has not said "Go," it's only because you're good where you are. You qualify, and you're good help so stay put!.

Elisha stayed with him, and in return Elijah said, "If you see me when I leave, you can have it." The mantle fell from Elijah, and Elisha looked up and saw him. He had to figure out where his help really came from. Elijah was caught up by fiery chariot and took off.

In my personal opinion, they're walking together when the fiery chariot came tearing through. When Elisha stood up he couldn't find Elijah. He looked up and he hollered, "Hey, Father!" and he said "I'm glad you looked up."

You can't look to a man or woman, you have to look to God. He will use a man or woman, but they are not the ones that give you power because they do not qualify. Elisha looked up, and when he started screaming, he threw off his mantle and picked up the new one.

People will say things like, "It's going to be cold after awhile," but you know it's alright because you're getting a new garment. Some will say, "Yeah but what if you need to go back to your waiter job?" You know it's alright, because you have a new job with new equipment now. When they ask you if you are sure, you know it's alright because you have a new job and a new mantle.

He ripped his mantle in half, threw it on the ground, and walked away to pick up the new mantle. He walked down to the creek, and he slapped the water with that mantle and shouted, "Where's the Lord, God of Elijah?" He knew how to slap the water because he watched his Man of God closely and paid attention.

1 Samuel 17:38

38And Saul armed David with his armour, and he put an helmet of brass upon his head; also he armed him with a coat of mail.

As David was getting cinched up, girded up and buttoned up in new armor, he turned to Saul thanked him, and declined his new equipment. He realized that he already had a mantle placed upon him from the beginning and that he already wore the right garment. He was appreciative and grateful, but recognized that God had already given him what he needed and was skilled with it.

Flattery will easily try to pull you away from God, but he leads by the Holy Ghost. Saul could have tried to compliment David to make him think more highly of himself, but David knew the anointing that was on his life.

God told me to follow different people when I didn't know come here from sick'em. I stayed under Kenneth E. Hagin until he left planet Earth. Then God told me and Sally to help build another church in Oklahoma. We just wanted to travel, but he told us to start another work. We could be invited to go to any state and we'd be thankful, but God told us to live in Pawnee, Oklahoma.

David recognized that the new armor did not represent what God called him to do, and it didn't fit him. He took it off, thanked Saul, and walked out of the tent honorably.

Battles never took place on a hilltop. The top men stayed on the hill on one side of a large valley and the enemy would be on a hill at the other side. David took off down the side of the hill and Goliath also made his way down into the valley.

I'm sure when David left the tent, they had little flags on poles flying in the wind with banners, and they had men on the other side scouting. He was not wearing a helmet like everybody else; he did not have escorts as other men did. He had his hands held high, and he was shouting as he was running.

When David arrived at the flat, the scouts on the other side were making fun of him. They thought he was no threat and simply a short shepherd boy unworthy of battle. Goliath went down to the flat, and David took off running to a brook to gather up stones. Goliath asked why they would send someone who didn't know how to fight, someone uneducated, and insult him by doing so.

David challenged him and used every bit of equipment he knew how to use. What David had was knowledge of the spirit. He knew that Goliath could come at him with a natural sword that could cut him, but he had the sword of the spirit. Goliath may not have seen the sword, but he felt it. David came at him with the mantle God put on his life. He wound up his weapon, flung a rock at Goliath and he fell. David walked over on him, and he said that the sword of the giant was so big that it looked like a weaver's beam.

David must have been in good shape, women chased after him. He picked up the sword, and he gets on top of the giant. He gets that sword up, and then he stands beside him. It doesn't say whether he's dead or if he's completely out, but the bible says he took the sword from Goliath.

Can you imagine what your enemy in the realm of the spirit does when they have shot you with everything they've got? They use their best arsenal, their best camp, their best warrior. You hit them with the word of God and stay in faith and then they fall. Then you take the sword of the spirit and you cut that thing's head off.

Can you imagine the chaos that happened up there on the side of that hill? They probably went bumping into each other in confusion and then left. David grabbed him by the hair on his head and raised it into the air. His head is bigger than the size of a basketball, and his eyes may have rolled back in his head when he cut him. He's standing there holding by the hair, the head of the thing that had tried to kill him.

That thing that tried to destroy you, if you stay where God put you, you learn to use your equipment to destroy it. Stay where God's asked you to, become skillful with what God's asked you to do, and you'll end up with that giant in your hand.